Let us start rebuilding...
The God of Heaven will give us
success.

NEHEMIAH 2:18, 20 NIV

JL GERHARDT

FRESH START
FRESH STRENGTH

Seeing God in Nehemiah

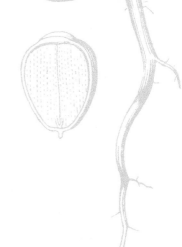

A LOOK TO LOVE BIBLE STUDY

Fresh Start. Fresh Strength.

Unless otherwise noted, all Scripture quotations are taken from the
Christian Standard Bible® Copyright © 2017 by Holman Bible
Publishers. Used by permission. Christian Standard Bible®, and CSB®
are federally registered trademarks of Holman Bible Publishers.

Paperback ISBN: 9798569870981

A NOTE

Hi!

JL here. Just wanted to take a moment and let you know how happy I am you decided to read the book of Nehemiah with me.

I wrote this study in the second half of 2020, more than six months into the COVID-19 pandemic. This is the year "dumpster fire" was officially added to the dictionary. With so many people I know having lost so much (health, jobs, relationships), I find myself looking to Israel. At the start of the book of Nehemiah, Israel was a nation in ruins, having lost her precious capital city, her national identity, her freedom, and, more significantly, her intimate relationship with God. It was a dark chapter in Israel's history, *but it wasn't the end of the story.*

In this season of rubble, I'm looking to Nehemiah for hope that perhaps things can be rebuilt. The more I read, the more convinced I am that God is always waiting for me with a fresh start and fresh strength.

God bless you (and strengthen you) as you read and as you make your own fresh start,

CONTENTS

Getting Started

Daily Reading Guides

Wrapping things up

Don't miss this!

WEEKLY TEACHING VIDEOS AVAILABLE AT JLGERHARDT.COM/FRESHSTART

Password:
mamasgotabrandnewwall

YOU'LL ALSO FIND A HELPFUL GROUP LEADER GUIDE

HOW TO USE THIS BOOK

This is not a book book. It doesn't have chapters or stories or long thoughtful essays. It's more like a guidebook, a tool for fully experiencing something else-- in this case, the Old Testament book of Nehemiah. I'll point out people and moments and sentences you shouldn't miss. I'll share favorite glimpses of God and offer new ways of understanding things you thought you already had figured out. I'll also ask lots of questions--questions to prod you, questions to push you, and questions to help you see. *To see the text. To see God in the text. And to see yourself--as you are and as you might one day be.*

This book is intended to be used in conjunction with both
1. Your personal reading of the book of Nehemiah *and*
2. The six teaching videos you'll find at jlgerhardt.com/freshstart

Don't skip the readings, and don't miss the videos! The very best things I've learned about God in Nehemiah are packed into those messages.

If you're using this book as an accessory to your personal study of Nehemiah, I recommend working your way through it in six weeks, watching the teaching videos after you've finished each week's set of daily reading guides. If you're using this book in a class, small group, or book club, I recommend taking 7-8 weeks (though six would do). Group leaders can find discussion guides and an 8 week plan at jlgerhardt.com/freshstart.

If you'd like to dive even deeper into the book of Nehemiah, consider one of the following extra challenges. Any one of them would greatly enhance your experience with God in the book:

1. Choose a verse (or set of verses) to memorize each week. By the time you're done, you'll have God's truth in Nehemiah taking root in your heart.
2. Handwrite the book of Nehemiah (or selected parts of it). Writing the Bible in my own handwriting helps me remember it!
3. Illustrate the book of Nehemiah. If words aren't your thing, sketch one illustration each week to express what you're learning about God's character.

God, our Father,

Giver of fresh starts and fresh strength,
We ask You to walk with us as we read Nehemiah together,
to open our eyes to wonders in Your Word,
to empower us to see You on the page,
to help us know You better and love You more.
God, be in every circumstance we carry into our reading.
God, whatever rubble we find in our lives, give us hope for rebuilding.
Be close to us as we mourn and inspire us to imagine a better future.
Show us how to depend on You when we're tired and sad and overwhelmed
by the mess of this fallen world. When it feels like there's too much wrong
and too much to fix and too much to carry,
be our Fresh Start and Fresh Strength.
God, for those of us studying Nehemiah with others,
use this time to draw us together. Bind us in our shared love for You
and our shared circumstances.
God, thank You for history, for books like Nehemiah, for true stories
reminding us of Who You are and who Your people are when they depend
on You. Help us hold our family story dear—
to learn it, to be shaped and inspired by it, and to tell it.
By the power of Jesus Christ we approach Your throne,

Amen.

WEEK 1

WEEK 1
Reading Guide

Monday	NEHEMIAH 1:1-3
Tuesday	NEHEMIAH 1:3-11
Wednesday	NEHEMIAH 1:5-11
Thursday	NEHEMIAH 2:1-10
Friday	NEHEMIAH 2:11-18

Over the course of this study we'll often read a passage two or three times.
Any repeats are intentional.

Day 1

FIRST, PRAY

God, open our eyes that we might see You in your Word.
Every day before we read, we'll pray this simple prayer. As I've spent time in scripture, I've found it to be enormously fruitful.

SECOND, READ

Nehemiah 1:1-3

> The words of Nehemiah son of Hacaliah:
> During the month of Chislev in the twentieth year, when I was in the fortress city of Susa, Hanani, one of my brothers, arrived with men from Judah, and I questioned them about Jerusalem and the Jewish remnant that had survived the exile. They said to me, "The remnant in the province, who survived the exile, are in great trouble and disgrace. Jerusalem's wall has been broken down, and its gates have been burned."

THIRD, LEARN

We can't understand the book of Nehemiah without talking about what comes before the book of Nehemiah (just as you can't really get tomorrow's fresh start without taking a moment to reflect on yesterday's mess).

Nehemiah (the man) is one in a series of leaders God will use to rebuild Israel after their fall to the Babylonians and exile in Babylon, later Persia. Nehemiah is (as we'll see in tomorrow's reading) a high level servant in the Persian king's court who will lead the charge to repair the walls of Jerusalem.

In the year 598 Babylon began their conquest of Judah (the Assyrians conquered the Northern Kingdom of Israel in 772 BC), making slaves of Judah's finest young men and women (including, for example, Daniel of lion's den fame). This conquest came after generations of disobedience on the part of God's people. When it became painfully obvious that Judah would not give up their idols and follow God's law, God turned them over to Babylon. Eventually, the nation would be fully conquered and even Solomon's temple in Jerusalem (perhaps the most beautiful building ever constructed, the seat of God's presence on earth) would be destroyed.

God's people, carted off to Babylon, uprooted from the Land of Promise, were devastated.

In Psalm 137 (NIV) we read,
> By the rivers of Babylon we sat and wept
> when we remembered Zion.
> There on the poplars we hung our harps,
> for there our captors asked us for songs,
> our tormentors demanded songs of joy;
> they said, "Sing us one of the songs of Zion!"
> How can we sing the songs of the Lord
> while in a foreign land?
> If I forget you, Jerusalem,
> may my right hand forget its skill.
> May my tongue cling to the roof of my mouth
> if I do not remember you,
> if I do not consider Jerusalem
> my highest joy.

When the book of Nehemiah opens, Israelites have lived in Babylon (now Persia) for more than 150 years—that's 5-6 generations. If you're an American, it's helpful to realize that 150 years ago was 1870. Ulysses Grant was president. The Brooklyn Bridge hadn't yet been built. If your people had lived in America for 150 years you would almost certainly consider yourself an American.

Nehemiah, though, doesn't consider himself Persian. Despite his high position in the king's court, despite his solid job, despite being born, raised, and schooled in Persia, Nehemiah considers himself an Israelite. *His heart is in Israel.*

He and his people are still singing this song:

> May my tongue cling to the roof of my mouth
> if I do not remember you,
> if I do not consider Jerusalem
> my highest joy.

For about 100 years, Israelites have been trying to rebuild their treasured city (often with the help of Persian kings). Read the book of Ezra (likely written by the same author as Nehemiah and originally included with Nehemiah as a single composition) and you'll see early efforts at rebuilding including the rebuilding of the temple. When Nehemiah gets the news that "the wall of Jerusalem is broken down, and its gates have been burned with fire," he weeps not for a Jerusalem long ago destroyed by the Babylonians, but rather a Jerusalem recently accosted by enemies of the rebuilding process.

FOURTH, REFLECT

We only read three verses today, but in those three verses we found plenty requiring explanation. Here's a quick definition of terms:

- "The month of Kislev" occurs during our November-December.
- "The citadel of Susa" is the palace of the Persian king (the same palace Esther lived in as queen). Ruins can be found today near the Iranian city of Shush.
- "The Jewish remnant" are the people who were not taken to Babylon during the exile. This was a small group of mostly poor and/or rural Israelites. As we mentioned already, Jerusalem is in the process of being rebuilt, and Nehemiah is looking for news on the progress.

As you consider these few verses, imagine you're living away from your homeland. A friend or brother arrives with devastating news: Your people are in "great trouble and disgrace." Take a moment to imagine what you'd be thinking and feeling. Write about it here:

While this text isn't "about us," there are things we can learn about our own circumstances from the text.

- Are you currently experiencing great trouble or disgrace? Has anything in your life been broken down or burned? Take a moment to survey the rubble and acknowledge the destruction. Don't walk away from this study today without writing down one place/relationship/routine/value/etc. in your life that's broken and needs to be rebuilt. Tomorrow we'll talk more about how to face that brokenness.

FIFTH, LOOK.

Where do you see God in today's passage?

We'll ask this question each day, but on no day will it be harder to answer than today—both because today's reading is so short and business-y AND because today's passage emerges from a world in which Israel has been banished from the presence of God.

If Israel is God's chosen nation, what can Israel's exile teach us about God? What kind of God lets His holy city fall into "great trouble and disgrace"? Take a minute to put together an answer.

Day 2

FIRST, PRAY

God, open our eyes that we might see You in your Word.
Empower us to mourn what's broken and burned down.
Turn us toward You in our grief.

SECOND, READ

Nehemiah 1:3-11

> They said to me, "The remnant in the province, who survived the exile, are in great trouble and disgrace. Jerusalem's wall has been broken down, and its gates have been burned."
>
> When I heard these words, I sat down and wept. I mourned for a number of days, fasting and praying before the God of the heavens. I said,
>
> Lord, the God of the heavens, the great and awe-inspiring God who keeps his gracious covenant with those who love him and keep his commands, let your eyes be open and your ears be attentive to hear your servant's prayer that I now pray to you day and night for your servants, the Israelites. I confess the sins we have committed against you. Both I and my father's family have sinned. We have acted corruptly toward you and have not kept the commands, statutes, and ordinances you gave your servant Moses. Please remember what you commanded your servant Moses: "If you are unfaithful, I will scatter you among the peoples. But if you return to me and carefully observe my commands, even though your exiles were banished to the farthest horizon, I will gather them from there and bring them to the place where I chose to have my name dwell." They are your servants and your people. You redeemed them by your great power and strong hand. Please, Lord, let your ear be attentive to the prayer of your servant and to that of your servants who delight to revere your name. Give your servant success today, and grant him compassion in the presence of this man.

At the time, I was the king's cupbearer.

THIRD, LEARN

Our reading today captures Nehemiah's reaction to the trouble and disgrace of Jerusalem. Notice, in his sadness, he doesn't eat some ice cream, distract himself with a hobby, and move on. Nehemiah instead embraces his sadness, sitting with it for "a number of days."

Mourning for the Jew was more than simply crying or being sad. Mourning was an intentional posture and spiritual practice in response to loss or hardship usually including weeping, fasting, some kind of material signal to the people around you (torn clothes or sackcloth), and prayer. In the Old Testament Israelites would mourn a death communally for thirty days. In the New Testament, John the Baptist's disciples appear to have practiced a form of mourning as they waited for the coming of the Messiah, fasting regularly.

Here we find Nehemiah mourning for Jerusalem.

FOURTH, REFLECT

Have you ever practiced mourning intentionally (with fasting, for a prescribed amount of time, etc.)? If so, what prompted it? Was it productive? If you haven't, why not?

What blessings might we find in sitting with (and expressing) our sadness?

We asked you yesterday to identify something in your life that's broken or burned down, something you'd like God's help rebuilding. Perhaps you picked your church. Maybe after this pandemic church just doesn't feel the same. Maybe you picked your marriage—maybe you're divorced. Maybe your marriage is just broken and you wish it wasn't but you don't know how to fix it. Maybe you picked a friendship or your bank account or your faith.

Before we jump ahead to the rebuilding phase, let's take a moment to mourn. What was beautiful about the thing you've lost? What hopes did you have that never materialized? Take a moment to meditate on the goodness of the past (or the hope for tomorrow that never bloomed into real life). It's okay if this makes you feel sad.

If this is truly something to mourn, consider fasting and praying for a prescribed amount of time. You might also gather others who've been affected by the loss and share your memories and pains.

One thing I love about Nehemiah's reaction to the trouble and disgrace in Jerusalem is this: His sadness turns him *toward* God and not *away* from God. Nehemiah prays as he mourns, because prayer and mourning belong together, because Nehemiah knows, "Even though I walk through the darkest valley... You are with me."

- Do you usually turn toward God or away from God in grief? When bad things happen do you want to pray or do you tend to avoid prayer?
- If you tend to turn away, why do you think that is?
- If you turn toward Him, why? What do you find when you seek Him in your sadness?

FIFTH, LOOK

Where do you see God in this passage?

What do you learn about God from the way Nehemiah interacts with God in his grief?

Day 3

FIRST, PRAY

God, open our eyes that we might see You in your Word.

When what we see in You and what we see in ourselves are at odds, convict us. Challenge us.

Empower us to see a better way and repent of our disobedience.

Remind us of Your unfailing compassion. Convince us we can always come home to You.

SECOND, READ

Nehemiah 1:5-11

I said,

Lord, the God of the heavens, the great and awe-inspiring God who keeps his gracious covenant with those who love him and keep his commands, let your eyes be open and your ears be attentive to hear your servant's prayer that I now pray to you day and night for your servants, the Israelites. I confess the sins we have committed against you. Both I and my father's family have sinned. We have acted corruptly toward you and have not kept the commands, statutes, and ordinances you gave your servant Moses. Please remember what you commanded your servant Moses: "If you are unfaithful, I will scatter you among the peoples. But if you return to me and carefully observe my commands, even though your exiles were banished to the farthest horizon, I will gather them from there and bring them to the place where I chose to have my name dwell." They are your servants and your people. You redeemed them by your great power and strong hand. Please, Lord, let your ear be attentive to the prayer of your servant and to that of your servants who delight to revere your name. Give your servant success today, and grant him compassion in the presence of this man.

At the time, I was the king's cupbearer.

THIRD, LEARN

For the last few months I've been studying the prophets, watching God warn Israel again and again to stop sinning against Him, to tear down their idols, and repent. If you read from Isaiah straight through to Malachi, you'll notice the same plot on repeat: Israel sins, God warns Israel, Israel sins some more despite the warning, God punishes Israel, Israel cries out, God gives Israel another chance, Israel sins... Wash, rinse, repeat.

As I read I can't help getting judge-y. How could Israel treat God like that? How could they turn away so many times? How could they... And then I realize how much like Israel we are, and I'm humbled. Humbled and immensely thankful. As Nehemiah says, our God is the "great and awesome God... who keeps his covenant of love" (NIV). When we turn away from Him He is always, always ready to welcome us back.

Here in his prayer, we find Nehemiah doing two things: 1. Confessing sin and 2. Reminding God of His promise to take Israel back. Let's not skip the first to grab hold of the second.

Yes, God is a God who forgives. Yes, "even though [His] exiled people were banished to the farthest horizon, [He] will gather them." But God wants repentance first. If we want a fresh start, we need to start like Nehemiah did—by owning our sin, confessing it, and turning away from it.

FOURTH, REFLECT

As you consider the broken and burned down places in your own life, are there any sins you need to confess, any way in which you may have contributed to the brokenness and destruction? What do you need to leave behind in order to get that fresh start with God? Spend some time in prayer today confessing your sins.

Often, we think of sin as something individual, a choice we made personally to disobey God. Nehemiah here hasn't sinned personally. Instead he's confessing Israel's collective sin. Consider spending some time confessing the collective sins of either your nation, your family, your church, or your organization. Perhaps you've unwittingly participated in those sins. Perhaps you benefit in some way from those sins. Take them to God humbly.

FIFTH, LOOK

Where do you see God in this passage?

Consider Nehemiah's prayer. Who is God according to Nehemiah? What does Nehemiah expect from God?

Have you ever experienced God's faithfulness to His covenant of love? When?

Day 4

FIRST, PRAY

God, open our eyes that we might see You in your Word.
Let Your gracious hand be on us.

SECOND, READ

Nehemiah 2:1-10

During the month of Nisan in the twentieth year of King Artaxerxes, when wine was set before him, I took the wine and gave it to the king. I had never been sad in his presence, so the king said to me, "Why do you look so sad, when you aren't sick? This is nothing but sadness of heart."

I was overwhelmed with fear and replied to the king, "May the king live forever! Why should I not be sad when the city where my ancestors are buried lies in ruins and its gates have been destroyed by fire?"

Then the king asked me, "What is your request?"

So I prayed to the God of the heavens and answered the king, "If it pleases the king, and if your servant has found favor with you, send me to Judah and to the city where my ancestors are buried, so that I may rebuild it."

The king, with the queen seated beside him, asked me, "How long will your journey take, and when will you return?" So I gave him a definite time, and it pleased the king to send me.

I also said to the king, "If it pleases the king, let me have letters written to the governors of the region west of the Euphrates River, so that they will grant me safe passage until I reach Judah. And let me have a letter written to Asaph, keeper of the king's forest, so that he will give me timber to rebuild the gates of the temple's fortress, the city wall, and the home where I will live." The king granted my requests, for the gracious hand of my God was on me.

I went to the governors of the region west of the Euphrates and gave them the king's letters. The king had also sent officers of the infantry and cavalry with me. When Sanballat the Horonite and Tobiah the Ammonite official heard that someone had come to pursue the prosperity of the Israelites, they were greatly displeased.

THIRD, LEARN

A few things to know about Nehemiah's job as cupbearer:

1. This is not a slave position. Nehemiah is a high ranking official in the court, well compensated and respected.
2. Nehemiah was both bodyguard and butler/sommelier. His job was to protect the king from being poisoned by overseeing the storage and service of the wine, occasionally drinking suspicious wine himself to be sure of the king's safety. As Persian kings drank and served a great deal of wine (to very important people and on very important occasions), Nehemiah's job would have required him to be alert, highly organized, and sophisticated (imagine Carson from *Downton Abbey*). In many courts the cupbearer was also expected to be physically beautiful—so as to up the "fanciness" of feasts and royal occasions.
3. Given his regular presence in court and intimacy with the king (they drank from the same cup), the cupbearer often served as an advisor to the King.

Why does this matter? It's valuable to realize the kind of man Nehemiah is. He's not a cowering servant, lowest on the totem pole, accustomed to being abused and overlooked. He's powerful, well-connected, and admired. And yet, we find him in this passage "overwhelmed with fear" and turning to God for strength.

When it's time to talk to the king about Israel, Nehemiah doesn't lean on his own abilities or past accomplishments for courage. He leans on God. And when he does: "The king granted my requests, for the gracious hand of my God was on me."

P.S It's interesting that Nehemiah lets 3-5 months pass before going to the king with his plan. Perhaps this is evidence of his fear. More likely it's evidence of Nehemiah's thorough preparation (This guys is totally an enneagram 1).

FOURTH, REFLECT

As you consider making a fresh start in some area of your life, are you depending on God's strength to make it happen? What would that look like to depend on God, practically speaking?

What keeps us from depending on God?

Nehemiah has big plans for Israel and asks the king of Persia for a lot of help—proof that Nehemiah is expecting God to show up. Consider your plans for rebuilding or your dreams for some coming project or relationship. Are you dreaming big? Do your dreams require the strength of God? Or are you keeping your dreams small to match your own strength?

What would it look like for you to dream a bigger dream?

FIFTH, LOOK

Where do you see God in this passage?

What does God accomplish?

What do you learn from Nehemiah about what you can ask from God?

Day 5

FIRST, PRAY

God, open our eyes that we might see You in your Word.
Enable us to see You in your graciousness to others.
Empower us to buy in when others try to lead us in your good work.

SECOND, READ

Nehemiah 2:11-18

After I arrived in Jerusalem and had been there three days, I got up at night and took a few men with me. I didn't tell anyone what my God had laid on my heart to do for Jerusalem. The only animal I took was the one I was riding. I went out at night through the Valley Gate toward the Serpent's Well and the Dung Gate, and I inspected the walls of Jerusalem that had been broken down and its gates that had been destroyed by fire. I went on to the Fountain Gate and the King's Pool, but farther down it became too narrow for my animal to go through. So I went up at night by way of the valley and inspected the wall. Then heading back, I entered through the Valley Gate and returned. The officials did not know where I had gone or what I was doing, for I had not yet told the Jews, priests, nobles, officials, or the rest of those who would be doing the work. So I said to them, "You see the trouble we are in. Jerusalem lies in ruins and its gates have been burned. Come, let's rebuild Jerusalem's wall, so that we will no longer be a disgrace." I told them how the gracious hand of my God had been on me, and what the king had said to me.

They said, "Let's start rebuilding," and their hands were strengthened to do this good work.

THIRD, LEARN

In our reading today, Nehemiah arrives in Jerusalem, lays low, examines the state of things, and convinces the Israelites living near the city of Jerusalem to join him in his effort to rebuild the walls.

Two things that stuck out to me:

1. Nehemiah takes his time getting to know the city, the people, and the problem before getting to work. Too often I rush into a project sure I know the best way to proceed only to encounter setback after setback, setbacks that could have been prevented had I slowed down and paid attention.
2. When it comes time to recruit the people of Jerusalem for rebuilding the walls, Nehemiah nails the presentation: He starts with what they all know and agree upon, "You see the trouble we are in," followed by a clear call to action, "Come, let's rebuild Jerusalem's wall," supported by proof that God is in support of the plan, "I told them how the gracious hand of my God had been on me." If you're ever looking to lead a group of God's people into action, this method could come in handy.

FOURTH, REFLECT

Are you rushing to rebuild or fix a problem right now? Have you taken time to examine what's broken? Have you made a plan for construction? What might it look like to slow down and pay attention? Identify 2 or 3 steps you could take to prepare.

Why is God's graciousness toward Nehemiah such an effective selling point for Nehemiah's plan?

Have you ever experienced the gracious hand of God? Have you considered sharing that story to encourage others to join with you in Kingdom work? How might you do that? Who needs to hear your story?

FIFTH, LOOK

Where do you see God in today's passage?

Personally, I'm zooming in on what Nehemiah's success with the king says about Who God is and how He acts.

Don't forget!

THIS WEEK'S TEACHING VIDEO AVAILABLE AT JLGERHARDT.COM/FRESHSTART

Password:
mamasgotabrandnewwall

WEEK 2

WEEK 2
Reading Guide

Monday	NEHEMIAH 2:19-20
Tuesday	NEHEMIAH 3:1-31
Wednesday	NEHEMIAH 4:1-5
Thursday	NEHEMIAH 4:6-14
Friday	NEHEMIAH 4:15-23

Day 1

FIRST, PRAY

God, open our eyes that we might see You in your Word.
Empower us to persevere in faith even in the face of opposition.

SECOND, READ

Nehemiah 2:19-20

> When Sanballat the Horonite, Tobiah the Ammonite official, and Geshem the Arab
> heard about this, they mocked and despised us, and said, "What is this you're doing? Are
> you rebelling against the king?" I gave them this reply, "The God of the heavens is the
> one who will grant us success. We, his servants, will start building, but you have no share,
> right, or historic claim in Jerusalem."

THIRD, LEARN

Sanballat, Tobiah, and Geshem—who are these guys and *how dare they?*

All three are leaders of regions and peoples adjacent to Judah and Jerusalem (awarded their
positions of power by the king of Persia—just like Nehemiah). Some scholars/historians
have identified them as anti-Jew, but Tobiah may be Jewish by birth and Sanballat will
attempt to marry his family line into the Jewish priesthood (more on that later). This is more
complicated than "they hated Jews." It's more likely they're concerned about losing power
over the region.

Sanballat lives in Samaria (perhaps he gets the nickname "the Horonite" from his likely
hometown: Horonaim in Moab). Tobiah is an Ammonite (though possibly he's simply been
given authority over the Ammonites and isn't one himself), and Geshem is an Arab.

Nehemiah, remember, is the new guy in town. These three are like the popular kids on the playground, trying to maintain their status by quickly putting newcomers in their place. Their opposition to Nehemiah's efforts will be a plague for the entirety of the effort.

FOURTH, REFLECT

You cannot do good work without running into opposition. Everything, everything, everything worth doing attracts haters.

So often today when Christians talk about following God and doing God's work we talk about open doors and miraculous coincidences and God-enabled ease. We say, everything fell into place; "it was such a God thing." I love it when that happens. But what we need to remember is that God doesn't only work in coincidence and open doors and easy paths. Sometimes God calls His people to locked doors and gives them the strength to knock them down.

If, in the work God's called you to, you experience opposition, don't waver. When the people who oppose God, oppose you, celebrate. You're doing something right.

Knowing that doesn't take away the sting. But it will prepare you for the inevitable and enable you to keep going.

- Where are you experiencing opposition in your efforts to do good work and follow God? Is it discouraging you?
- How might you respond to that opposition?

FIFTH, LOOK

Where do you see God in today's passage?

Let's look for God in Nehemiah's response to ridicule: "The God of the heavens is the one who will grant us success. We, his servants, will start building, but you have no share, right, or historic claim in Jerusalem."

- What makes Nehemiah so confident?
- What do we learn about God from the preferential treatment He gives His servants?

Day 2

FIRST, PRAY

God, open our eyes that we might see You in your Word.
Bring us partners in the work You're calling us to do, or make us partners in the good work
You're calling someone else to lead.

SECOND, READ

Nehemiah 3:1-31
We won't include the whole reading here today—you'll need to grab your Bible. Instead,
we've featured a highlight (verses 17-32).

> Next to him the Levites made repairs under Rehum son of Bani. Beside him Hashabiah,
> ruler of half the district of Keilah, made repairs for his district. After him their fellow
> Levites made repairs under Binnui son of Henadad, ruler of half the district of Keilah.
> Next to him Ezer son of Jeshua, ruler of Mizpah, made repairs to another section
> opposite the ascent to the armory at the Angle.
>
> After him Baruch son of Zabbai diligently repaired another section, from the Angle to
> the door of the house of the high priest Eliashib. Beside him Meremoth son of Uriah, son
> of Hakkoz, made repairs to another section, from the door of Eliashib's house to the end
> of his house. And next to him the priests from the surrounding area made repairs. After
> them Benjamin and Hasshub made repairs opposite their house. Beside them Azariah
> son of Maaseiah, son of Ananiah, made repairs beside his house. After him Binnui son of
> Henadad made repairs to another section, from the house of Azariah to the Angle and
> the corner. Palal son of Uzai made repairs opposite the Angle and tower that juts out
> from the king's upper palace, by the courtyard of the guard. Beside him Pedaiah son of
> Parosh and the temple servants living on Ophel made repairs opposite the Water Gate
> toward the east and the tower that juts out. Next to him the Tekoites made repairs to
> another section from a point opposite the great tower that juts out, as far as the wall of
> Ophel.

Each of the priests made repairs above the Horse Gate, each opposite his own house. After them Zadok son of Immer made repairs opposite his house. And beside him Shemaiah son of Shecaniah, guard of the East Gate, made repairs. Next to him Hananiah son of Shelemiah and Hanun the sixth son of Zalaph made repairs to another section. After them Meshullam son of Berechiah made repairs opposite his room. Next to him Malchijah, one of the goldsmiths, made repairs to the house of the temple servants and the merchants, opposite the Inspection Gate, and as far as the upstairs room on the corner. The goldsmiths and merchants made repairs between the upstairs room on the corner and the Sheep Gate.

THIRD, LEARN

Some interesting facts about the men (and women!) rebuilding the walls:
- They're a motley crew. Wall builders come from all rungs of the economic ladder—rulers build right alongside servants and priests. Professions represented: perfume maker, Levite, district ruler, governor, merchant, guard, servant, goldsmith, and priest. We even have the daughters of Shallum jumping in to help their father.
- They take responsibility for varying amounts of work. Some (like Shallun in vs 15) take on a few big projects. Some only commit to repairing their own house built into the wall. Each worker is necessary, even the ones who only do a little.
- They build together, at the same time, next to one another. They don't take turns or work at their own pace. "Together" seems to be hugely important in maintaining morale, instilling courage, and inspiring quick work.

FOURTH, REFLECT

We'll talk in this week's teaching video about the power of partnership. Partnership is more important than ever given culture's increasing embrace of isolation. There are things that MUST be done that CANNOT be done alone, and the more we pull away from one another, the less we're able to do/make/build/pursue big things.

Have you ever been a part of a project like rebuilding Jerusalem's wall? Something you could never do alone? How did it feel? What was delightful about that kind of devoted partnership? What was challenging?

What do you think prevents us from partnering more?

Do you have a project you're working on that requires more than you can give? What would it look like for you to recruit partners?

Are you craving meaningful work? How might you go about looking for a project to join as a partner?

FIFTH, LOOK

Where do you see God in this passage?

We don't have an explicit mention of God in chapter 3, but that doesn't mean He's not there. What happens in chapter 3 that could only happen by the grace of God?

Day 3

FIRST, PRAY

God, open our eyes that we might see You in your Word.
Hear us when we are despised. Defeat those who would stop us from doing the good You've called us to do.

SECOND, READ

Nehemiah 4:1-5

> When Sanballat heard that we were rebuilding the wall, he became furious. He mocked the Jews before his colleagues and the powerful men of Samaria and said, "What are these pathetic Jews doing? Can they restore it by themselves? Will they offer sacrifices? Will they ever finish it? Can they bring these burnt stones back to life from the mounds of rubble?" Then Tobiah the Ammonite, who was beside him, said, "Indeed, even if a fox climbed up what they are building, he would break down their stone wall!"

> Listen, our God, for we are despised. Make their insults return on their own heads and let them be taken as plunder to a land of captivity. Do not cover their guilt or let their sin be erased from your sight, because they have angered the builders.

THIRD, LEARN

Sanballat and the boys are back at it, ridiculing Israel and otherwise doing their best to discourage the building team. Interesting fact: Sanballat means "bramble-bush" or "enemy in secret" in Hebrew. Eberhard Schrader, student of ancient near east languages, considered that the name in the Akkadian language was Sīnuballit, from the name of the

Sumerian moon god Sīn, meaning "Sīn has begotten." It's possible his birth name was "Sinballit" and the Jews called him "Sanballat."

All of this is easily found via Google—just be sure when googling to check a few sources and make sure they match up.

Another interesting fact: The fox Tobiah mentions is probably the sand fox—likely the most common fox in that time and place and an especially small animal (even among foxes it's itty bitty) with padded feet that help distribute its weight on sand so that it barely affects whatever it walks on. *The insult is even worse than it seems at first glance.*

FOURTH, REFLECT

According to today's reading, when insulted the wall builders respond in two ways:
1. They pray.
2. They work with all their hearts.

Which one's harder for you when you run into opposition? Prayer? Or digging in and doing the work with all your heart? Why do you think that is?

Are you quick to pray when you run into trouble? Or do you jump to fixing it yourself first? Think of an example.

When's the last time you worked with all your heart on something important? Write a little about how it felt.

FIFTH, LOOK

Where do you see God in this passage?

What is Nehemiah asking God to do here? Why does Nehemiah feel like that's an acceptable thing to ask?

Are we allowed to ask for the downfall of our enemies? Is God cool with that?

One more thing! I don't want to miss this insult from Sanballat: "Can they bring the stones back to life from those heaps of rubble—burned as they are?" He assumes the answer is no here. Obviously. But we know better. We know Jesus says (standing in this very city, looking at this very temple), "Destroy this temple, and I will raise it again in three days." He's talking about His body—yes, but He's also declaring His general resurrection power. God is the God who brings stones back to life.

- What is God bringing back to life for you right now? What do you need to let Him bring back to life?

Day 4

FIRST, PRAY

God, open our eyes that we might see You in your Word.
Show us when and how to fight.

SECOND, READ

Nehemiah 4:6-14

So we rebuilt the wall until the entire wall was joined together up to half its height, for the people had the will to keep working.

When Sanballat, Tobiah, and the Arabs, Ammonites, and Ashdodites heard that the repair to the walls of Jerusalem was progressing and that the gaps were being closed, they became furious. They all plotted together to come and fight against Jerusalem and throw it into confusion. So we prayed to our God and stationed a guard because of them day and night.

In Judah, it was said:
> The strength of the laborer fails,
> since there is so much rubble.
> We will never be able
> to rebuild the wall.

And our enemies said, "They won't realize it until we're among them and can kill them and stop the work." When the Jews who lived nearby arrived, they said to us time and again, "Everywhere you turn, they attack us." So I stationed people behind the lowest sections of the wall, at the vulnerable areas. I stationed them by families with their swords, spears, and bows. After I made an inspection, I stood up and said to the nobles, the officials, and the rest of the people, "Don't be afraid of them. Remember the great and awe-inspiring Lord, and fight for your countrymen, your sons and daughters, your wives and homes."

THIRD, LEARN

In verse 8 we see Sanballat and his crew threatening action against Jerusalem. In verse 9 Nehemiah responds with a simple 2 part plan: pray and post a guard. We can assume Nehemiah felt perfectly comfortable with this plan and wouldn't have done much more. BUT. The people start talking...

- *In Judah it was said*, "The strength of the laborer fails, since there is so much rubble. We will never be able to rebuild the wall." (based on formatting, this appears to be either a song or or poem, maybe some kind of chant).
- *Also our enemies said*, "They won't realize it until we're among them and can kill them and stop the work."
- *When the Jews who lived nearby arrived, they said to us time and again*, "Everywhere you turn, they attack us."

Is it true that the people can't rebuild the wall because of the rubble? Not at all. They're halfway done already. And (spoiler alert) we'll soon see them finish in a remarkable 52 days. The people in Judah aren't making a report based on facts. They're expressing fear based on feelings. They *feel* like the wall can't be rebuilt.

Is it true that the enemies will kill them? We can't know for sure whether or not this threat is legit, but we do know Sanballat and his crew do not attack Jerusalem and no one dies at the hands of Jerusalem's enemies. These are ultimately empty threats. But that doesn't mean they don't have a huge affect on morale.

Finally, what about these Jews who're terrified that the wall-building is going to leave them vulnerable to attack? It doesn't. They're fine. Freaked out. But fine.

BTW These Jews living outside the city aren't helping rebuild the wall; they're just watching. But when did that stop anybody from having strong opinions?

This is the point in the task when everyone starts whining. Nehemiah, doer of good work, is threatened by outsiders, worn down by insiders, and accosted by bystanders. So, what does a good leader do when the team threatens to quit? Here's what Nehemiah does:

- He encourages families to work alongside one another. He wants everyone building beside someone they love, someone they'd fight for.

- Next, he "look[s] things over." He pauses, reconsiders, weighs his choices, and listens to input. When he's done looking things over, he's sure. The plan is good. Buck up, team. Back to work!
- But first, a good, inspiring speech—a St Crispin's Day speech, William Wallace to the troops, Coach Dale to the team in Hoosiers:

I stood up and said to the nobles, the officials, and the rest of the people, "Don't be afraid of them. Remember the great and awe-inspiring Lord, and fight for your countrymen, your sons and daughters, your wives and homes."

Nehemiah tells his people, Remember God, the God who never gives up on us, the God who fights for us. AND Don't give up on your people. Fight for what you love.

FOURTH, REFLECT

What, in your life, is worth fighting for? Where might God be calling you to put up a fight?

Nehemiah and his men carried spears and swords; what weapons can you use to fight for your family and your home (for whatever good thing you're trying to do)?

Christians usually think of themselves as people of peace, forgiving our enemies and all that good stuff. Is this call to fight relevant to us? Or is it outdated?

FIFTH, LOOK.

Where do you see God in today's passage?

Nehemiah says, "Don't be afraid of them. Remember the great and awe-inspiring Lord, and fight for your countrymen, your sons and daughters, your wives and homes."

- What's the connection between remembering the Lord and fighting?
- Why/how does remembering the Lord inspire bravery/action?
- Name someone who remembered the Lord and was inspired to fight bravely (someone mentioned in the Bible, someone from history, someone you know…).

Day 5

FIRST, PRAY

God, open our eyes that we might see You in your Word.
Teach us to depend on You, and teach us to work.

SECOND, READ

Nehemiah 4:15-23

When our enemies heard that we knew their scheme and that God had frustrated it, every one of us returned to his own work on the wall. From that day on, half of my men did the work while the other half held spears, shields, bows, and armor. The officers supported all the people of Judah, who were rebuilding the wall. The laborers who carried the loads worked with one hand and held a weapon with the other. Each of the builders had his sword strapped around his waist while he was building, and the one who sounded the ram's horn was beside me. Then I said to the nobles, the officials, and the rest of the people, "The work is enormous and spread out, and we are separated far from one another along the wall. Wherever you hear the sound of the ram's horn, rally to us there. Our God will fight for us!" So we continued the work, while half of the men were holding spears from daybreak until the stars came out. At that time, I also said to the people, "Let everyone and his servant spend the night inside Jerusalem, so that they can stand guard by night and work by day." And I, my brothers, my servants, and the men of the guard with me never took off our clothes. Each carried his weapon, even when washing.

THIRD, LEARN

Clearly Nehemiah is taking the threat of violence seriously. He accepts a slowdown to the work, and he arms not just the guards but also the wall builders. He makes a plan for alerting the entire city should an attack take place. He doesn't even take a shower or undress for bed (to ensure he's never unprepared for the enemy). Builders and guards work on the wall from sun up to sun down, swords at their sides.

At the same time, Nehemiah is clearly depending on God—he gives God credit for frustrating the enemy's plan, and tells the people, "Our God will fight for us!"

One of the biggest lessons we can learn from Nehemiah, one of the things I've been so thankful to learn from this book, is that trusting in God and working hard are partners, not opposites.

Soapbox time: When I people talk about trusting in God's plan they often use words like wait or hold on or "be still." Then they quote Psalm 46, "Be still, and know that I am God" or Exodus 14:14 "The Lord will fight for you; you need only to be still." Their point? God only works when we stop our work and let Him do His.

Which is kinda true, *but not really.*

Do you know what Exodus 14:15 says? "Then the Lord said to Moses, 'Why are you crying out to me? Tell the Israelites to move on.'" Moses tells the Israelites to be still (best translated, "stop freaking out and trust"), and God says "Move on."

Moses and God are not in disagreement.

Yes, we do need to let go of our own selfish ambitions. We can't make God work our personal plan. But "be still" isn't about stopping; it's about trusting. And you can trust and work at the same time.

Let's get to it.

FOURTH, REFLECT

Which comes easier to you, trusting God or showing up for hard work? It's cool if you're good at both (Nehemiah is). Why do you think you lean the way you do?

What ditch do we find on each end of the spectrum? What's the problem with "trusting God" but not working? What's the problem with hard work and no trust?

Nehemiah takes his enemy seriously. Are you taking your enemy seriously? What are you doing to protect yourself against the forces of evil? What would it look like to build with a sword at your side?

FIFTH, LOOK

Where do you see God in today's passage?

What do you think? Is God here? Who looks like God's conduit of grace in this passage?

CHECK OUT THIS WEEK'S TEACHING VIDEO FOR MORE ON
PARTNERSHIP AND DEALING WITH OPPOSITION.
JLGERHARDT.COM/FRESHSTART

WEEK 3

WEEK 3
Reading Guide

Monday	NEHEMIAH 5:1-13
Tuesday	NEHEMIAH 5:14-19
Wednesday	NEHEMIAH 6:1-14
Thursday	NEHEMIAH 6:15-7:3
Friday	NEHEMIAH 7:4-73

Day 1

FIRST, PRAY

God, open our eyes that we might see You in your Word.
Help us to help our brothers and sisters, to always lift others up and never lift ourselves up by pushing others down.

SECOND, READ

Nehemiah 5:1-13

There was a widespread outcry from the people and their wives against their Jewish countrymen. Some were saying, "We, our sons, and our daughters are numerous. Let us get grain so that we can eat and live." Others were saying, "We are mortgaging our fields, vineyards, and homes to get grain during the famine." Still others were saying, "We have borrowed money to pay the king's tax on our fields and vineyards. We and our children are just like our countrymen and their children, yet we are subjecting our sons and daughters to slavery. Some of our daughters are already enslaved, but we are powerless because our fields and vineyards belong to others."

I became extremely angry when I heard their outcry and these complaints. After seriously considering the matter, I accused the nobles and officials, saying to them, "Each of you is charging his countrymen interest." So I called a large assembly against them and said, "We have done our best to buy back our Jewish countrymen who were sold to foreigners, but now you sell your own countrymen, and we have to buy them back." They remained silent and could not say a word. Then I said, "What you are doing isn't right. Shouldn't you walk in the fear of our God and not invite the reproach of our foreign enemies? Even I, as well as my brothers and my servants, have been lending them money and grain. Please, let's stop charging this interest. Return their fields, vineyards, olive groves, and houses to them immediately, along with the percentage of the money, grain, new wine, and fresh oil that you have been assessing them."

They responded, "We will return these things and require nothing more from them. We will do as you say."

So I summoned the priests and made everyone take an oath to do this. I also shook the folds of my robe and said, "May God likewise shake from his house and property everyone who doesn't keep this promise. May he be shaken out and have nothing!"

The whole assembly said, "Amen," and they praised the Lord. Then the people did as they had promised.

THIRD, LEARN

In today's reading we encounter yet another hurdle to building the wall around Jerusalem. Some members of the Jewish community are suffering the effects of famine more significantly than others. The farmers (especially) are struggling and the bankers are getting rich off the farmers' bad luck. We find out in verses 1-5 that some Israelites have even sold their children in order to buy grain.

The main reason these farmers are struggling is that they're caught in a debt cycle. They borrow money because they don't have money but the bankers charge them to borrow money, putting them deeper in debt. You understand this if you've ever been so poor you had to put a pizza on a credit card. If you couldn't afford the ten dollars to buy the pizza, you certainly can't afford the $100 you'll pay for that pizza in payments and interest over the course of five years.

What's so shocking about this is that God had expressly forbidden Jews from charging interest on loans to fellow Jews:

- "If you lend silver to my people, to the poor person among you, you must not be like a creditor to him; you must not charge him interest.." Exodus 22:25
- "Do not profit or take interest from him, but fear your God and let your brother live among you.." Leviticus 25:36
- "Do not charge your brother interest on silver, food, or anything that can earn interest.." Deuteronomy 23:19

Despite the law against it, here Israel is charging interest, using their poor brothers and sisters to make themselves rich.

I find it so interesting that this chapter comes right on the heels of our discussion of partnership, of fighting alongside one another for a common goal. Nehemiah recognizes immediately that these people can't be partners if they're using one another for personal gain. Nehemiah tells the gathered builders, We're trying to do something here and you're off selling your own people to the Arabs and Moabites. Stop it.

Actually, Nehemiah doesn't just tell them to stop it, he tells them to fix it. *Stop the interest. Give back what you've taken. Make it right.*

And they do.: "The whole assembly said, "Amen," and they praised the Lord. Then the people did as they had promised." [I LOVE that line.]

FOURTH, REFLECT

There's so much to learn from this passage about how God's people should function in community. The big thing I want us to see is this: God's people don't push others down to lift themselves up.

Ever.

Instead, when some of God's people are down, God's other people lift them up.

God's people share. They share power. They share resources. They share access. If it's needed, and they have it, they share it.

You don't have enough. Here's enough. Repay me if you can, when you can. No worries. No hurry.

If what I have could bless you, it's yours.

Why do they share? Because they're partners. Because one person's good is everyone's good. And one person's pain is everyone's pain.

Next to him. Next to him. Next to him…

Nehemiah reminds the Israelites, we're all in this together.

- Is this a message you need to hear? Are you usually a good partner? Do you try to lift others up in partnership or are you more focused on your own needs? Think of a time you've partnered with others and reflect on how it went.

- Have you ever (in your lack) been pushed down by someone with plenty? Think of a specific example. How did that feel?
- Have you ever been lifted up (in your lack) by someone with plenty who was eager to share? How did that feel?

- What are you doing in your community of faith to make sure the resources are shared? Are there ways you could better empower those without power/wealth/education/etc?

These few verses might also have you considering debt and justice. If you're interested in ways today's Christians can fight against unjust and predatory lending practices, check out Faith for Just Lending (lendjustly.com), Christians of all stripes advocating for legislation against predators and justice for borrowers.

Finally, remember not all "debt" is financial. We have plenty of ways of enslaving or debasing one another.
- What's another way we might sabotage our mission by mistreating our partners? Specific examples encouraged!

FIFTH, LOOK

Where do you see God in today's passage?

What do we learn about Who God is and what He wants from his laws against interest? Why would God forbid that?

Day 2

FIRST, PRAY

God, open our eyes that we might see You in your Word.
God, help us to go first in sharing, to be an example, to accept less so others can have plenty.

SECOND, READ

Nehemiah 5:14-19

Furthermore, from the day King Artaxerxes appointed me to be their governor in the land of Judah—from the twentieth year until his thirty-second year, twelve years—I and my associates never ate from the food allotted to the governor. The governors who preceded me had heavily burdened the people, taking from them food and wine as well as a pound of silver. Their subordinates also oppressed the people, but because of the fear of God, I didn't do this. Instead, I devoted myself to the construction of this wall, and all my subordinates were gathered there for the work. We didn't buy any land.

There were 150 Jews and officials, as well as guests from the surrounding nations at my table. Each day, one ox, six choice sheep, and some fowl were prepared for me. An abundance of all kinds of wine was provided every ten days. But I didn't demand the food allotted to the governor, because the burden on the people was so heavy. Remember me favorably, my God, for all that I have done for this people.

THIRD, LEARN

One of the rules of the empire is this: everyone in charge takes a cut. When a citizen makes money, the king takes a cut, the governor takes a cut, the governor's assistants take a cut, and the person who collects the tax takes a cut. However much money you made is much less money after all's said and done.

As we learned last week, the people living in and around Jerusalem are struggling due to famine. There's simply not enough food to go around. It's Nehemiah's right as governor to take money (or food or land) from the people to pay himself and to pay his assistants. But Nehemiah says, "because of the fear of God, I didn't do this."

Not only does Nehemiah not take a salary for this work, he generously feeds 150 people from his own table.

Why? Is Nehemiah's work unworthy of compensation? Does he not deserve to be paid?

Nehemiah says, "I didn't demand the food allotted to the governor, because the burden on the people was so heavy." In other words, Nehemiah has compassion, and he does what he can to help those who need help.

I don't think this passage is about whether or not leaders deserve to be paid. I think it's about what leadership looks like when the people you're leading are suffering. Nehemiah has enough, extra even. We know this because he's able to generously feed 150 people night after night from his own wealth. Nehemiah is rich.

Because he has plenty, and because he's a partner, Nehemiah shares what he has for the good of the team.

That's leadership. *That's what Jesus will do in just a few hundred years.*

FOURTH, REFLECT

- Have you ever seen a leader act like Nehemiah does here? Take a moment to write about it. What did they do? Why did it matter? How did witnessing their generous compassion shape or challenge you?

- Are there things you're entitled to that God might be asking you to give up for the good of others?

FIFTH, LOOK

Where do you see God in today's passage?

Hint: Look at Nehemiah. What similarities do you see between Nehemiah and Jesus?

Day 3

FIRST, PRAY

God, open our eyes that we might see You in your Word.
Help us see what work matters most and devote ourselves to it no matter what.
Strengthen our hands.

SECOND, READ

Nehemiah 6:1-14

> When Sanballat, Tobiah, Geshem the Arab, and the rest of our enemies heard that I had rebuilt the wall and that no gap was left in it—though at that time I had not installed the doors in the city gates— Sanballat and Geshem sent me a message: "Come, let's meet together in the villages of the Ono Valley." They were planning to harm me.
>
> So I sent messengers to them, saying, "I am doing important work and cannot come down. Why should the work cease while I leave it and go down to you?" Four times they sent me the same proposal, and I gave them the same reply.
>
> Sanballat sent me this same message a fifth time by his aide, who had an open letter in his hand. In it was written:
>
>> It is reported among the nations—and Geshem agrees—that you and the Jews plan to rebel. This is the reason you are building the wall. According to these reports, you are to become their king and have even set up the prophets in Jerusalem to proclaim on your behalf, "There is a king in Judah." These rumors will be heard by the king. So come, let's confer together.
>
> Then I replied to him, "There is nothing to these rumors you are spreading; you are inventing them in your own mind." For they were all trying to intimidate us, saying, "They will drop their hands from the work, and it will never be finished."

But now, my God, strengthen my hands.

I went to the house of Shemaiah son of Delaiah, son of Mehetabel, who was restricted to his house. He said:
>Let's meet at the house of God,
>inside the temple.
>Let's shut the temple doors
>because they're coming to kill you.
>They're coming to kill you tonight!

But I said, "Should a man like me run away? How can someone like me enter the temple and live? I will not go." I realized that God had not sent him, because of the prophecy he spoke against me. Tobiah and Sanballat had hired him. He was hired, so that I would be intimidated, do as he suggested, sin, and get a bad reputation, in order that they could discredit me.

My God, remember Tobiah and Sanballat for what they have done, and also the prophetess Noadiah and the other prophets who wanted to intimidate me.

THIRD, LEARN

And the opposition continues...

At this point, Sanballat, Tobiah, and Gershom have realized they cannot defeat the army of men and women building the city via a direct attack, and with the walls so close to finished (only gates remain) they know time's running out. Their final play is to target Nehemiah, doing all they can to draw him away from his people or cause him to act in a way that might suggest he's weak or afraid. They try to arrange a meeting outside the city (surely an assassination attempt). They start rumors about him hoping the Persian king might hear the rumors or maybe hoping Nehemiah will feel the need to return to the king to clear up the rumors. Then they pay a prophet to lie to him, hoping he'll be so afraid he hides in the temple (embarrassing himself in front of the people and weakening the Israelite resolve). Each time, Nehemiah responds with bold certainty:

- To the call for a meeting Nehemiah says, "I am doing important work and cannot come down." They try to distract, and Nehemiah responds with increased focus.

- To the rumors Nehemiah says, "There is nothing to these rumors you are spreading; you are inventing them in your own mind." They try to intimidate, and Nehemiah responds unfazed.
- To the mercenary prophet Nehemiah says, "Should a man like me run away?" They try to make Nehemiah look frightened, and Nehemiah responds with confident courage.

The end is so close Nehemiah can smell it; this is not the time for weakness--which is why he prays to God, "But now, my God, strengthen my hands."

FOURTH, REFLECT

These fourteen verses we're reading today are full of wisdom. We'll spend some time in this week's teaching video focusing on verses 1-4 and Nehemiah's unrelenting focus. When he says "I am doing an important work and cannot come down," I am inspired to find my wall and not let anyone distract me from it.

What is it for you? What's your important work? What wall needs your attention and focus right now?

What does it look like specifically for you to do your important work? What are the tasks involved?

What would it look like to prioritize this work? What changes do you need to make?

What's tempting you to come down from your important work? What distractions do you need to reject?

Who are you going to ask to keep you accountable—to help keep you focused on your important work?

Also in this passage I don't want to miss Nehemiah's answer to the false prophet:

> *"Should a man like me run away? Or should someone like me go into the temple to save his life? I will not go!"*

At first glance this seems arrogant, but the more I read it, the more sure I am that this is exactly the kind of confidence anyone following God should have. Who is Nehemiah? He's a servant of Jehovah, God Almighty, Lord of angel armies. Nehemiah is a man of character. Nehemiah is faithful and focused. Nehemiah isn't someone who disobeys his God. Nehemiah isn't someone who hides from opposition.

Nehemiah is able to reject the schemes of the enemy because Nehemiah knows who he is.

The next time I'm tried by enemies, in the flesh or unseen, I want to have the guts to say, shoulders back, chin forward, "Should a woman like me run away?"

- Do you feel confident in your identity in Christ? Who are you, really? Take a moment to reflect on the power God's given you. If you're not living into your identity as God's servant, pray. Ask God to give you power and boldness.

FIFTH, LOOK

Where do you see God in today's passage?

Let's keep those eyes on Nehemiah as he walks with swagger in his holy calling.
- What's God enabling in this guy?
- What does God's work in Nehemiah's life and character teach us about God's priorities?

Day 4

FIRST, PRAY

God, open our eyes that we might see You in your Word.
Carry us on to completion.

SECOND, READ

Nehemiah 6:15-7:3

The wall was completed in fifty-two days, on the twenty-fifth day of the month Elul.
When all our enemies heard this, all the surrounding nations were intimidated and lost
their confidence, for they realized that this task had been accomplished by our God.

During those days, the nobles of Judah sent many letters to Tobiah, and Tobiah's letters
came to them. For many in Judah were bound by oath to him, since he was a son-in-law
of Shecaniah son of Arah, and his son Jehohanan had married the daughter of
Meshullam son of Berechiah. These nobles kept mentioning Tobiah's good deeds to me,
and they reported my words to him. And Tobiah sent letters to intimidate me.

When the wall had been rebuilt and I had the doors installed, the gatekeepers, singers,
and Levites were appointed. Then I put my brother Hanani in charge of Jerusalem, along
with Hananiah, commander of the fortress, because he was a faithful man who feared
God more than most. I said to them, "Do not open the gates of Jerusalem until the sun is
hot, and let the doors be shut and securely fastened while the guards are on duty. Station
the citizens of Jerusalem as guards, some at their posts and some at their homes."

THIRD, LEARN

It's done! Together, Nehemiah and the Israelites worked non-stop for 52 days, less than two months. It's both not much time at all and a lifetime given the conditions. Verse 16 helps us understand the scale of this success. Only with God could a thing like this be accomplished.

Even still, Tobiah hasn't given up trying to thwart Nehemiah's leadership. Turns out Tobiah has family connections inside the walls, including one of the wall builders. From *Ellicott's Commentary for English Readers*:

> Shechaniah was of the family of Arah, which had come over [to Israel from Persia] with Zerubbabel (Ezra 2:5). Tobiah had married his daughter, and Tobiah's son had married a daughter of Meshullam, one of the builders of the wall (Nehemiah 3:4; Nehemiah 3:30). This family connection led to a conspiracy by oath to thwart the governor. The names of Tobiah and his son are Hebrew; and it is probable that, though naturalised Ammonites, they were of Hebrew extraction. This renders it easier to understand the facility with which the affinity was contracted.

We can't know if Tobiah married the daughter of a high-ranking Israelite intentionally to grab power, but we do know it came in handy later. Unfortunately for Tobiah, he never was able to turn the connection into a coup.

This is the first glimpse we get at intermarriage between the Israelites/people of Judah and the inhabitants of the surrounding nations. We'll soon see how God feels about it.

FOURTH, REFLECT

Today's reading has me wondering, when do they celebrate finishing the wall? Seems like Nehemiah skips over that part, moving on to staffing logistics. As I read ahead, I do find a celebration on the horizon—but it's still six chapters away. Evidently Nehemiah isn't quite ready to call it a wrap.

As we reflect today let's focus on verse 16: "When all our enemies heard about this, all the surrounding nations were afraid and lost their self-confidence, because they realized that this work had been done with the help of our God."

- What work has God done through you that makes no sense outside of God's power? In other words, Is God working in you in unexplainable and remarkable ways? (Hint: If you're walking with Him, He is.)

Here's something I know: God is at work in His people.

Paul writes to the Philippian Christians: I am "confident of this, that he who began a good work in you will carry it on to completion until the day of Christ Jesus." A couple verses later he describes the work God's doing in His people, praying "that your love may abound more and more in knowledge and depth of insight, so that you may be able to discern what is best and may be pure and blameless for the day of Christ, filled with the fruit of righteousness that comes through Jesus Christ—to the glory and praise of God" (1:6-11, NIV).

God is growing His people in love, in knowledge, and in discernment. He's making them pure and blameless. He's filling them with the fruit of righteousness. And He's doing all of it, why? To His glory and praise.

Just like God strengthened Nehemiah and his team so that the outside nations would recognize His power, God is doing work in you for the purpose of His own glory

Is it obvious to others that what's good about you comes from God? Do others regularly give God credit for your achievements/growth/delightfulness? Why or why not?

How might we get out of God's way when it comes to receiving the glory? Are there practical steps we can take?

FIFTH, LOOK

Where do you see God in today's passage?

Maybe look at the men Nehemiah appoints to leadership. Is God in them?

Certainly we can see God in the completion of the wall. Even the surrounding nations could see God in an accomplishment like that.

Day 5

FIRST, PRAY

God, open our eyes that we might see You in your Word.
Enable us to get busy.

SECOND, READ

Nehemiah 7:4-73
Today's reading is loooong. Here's a glimpse (verses 4-18)

The city was large and spacious, but there were few people in it, and no houses had been built yet. Then my God put it into my mind to assemble the nobles, the officials, and the people to be registered by genealogy. I found the genealogical record of those who came back first, and I found the following written in it:

These are the people of the province who went up among the captive exiles deported by King Nebuchadnezzar of Babylon. Each of them returned to Jerusalem and Judah, to his own town. They came with Zerubbabel, Jeshua, Nehemiah, Azariah, Raamiah, Nahamani, Mordecai, Bilshan, Mispereth, Bigvai, Nehum, and Baanah.
The number of the Israelite men included
Parosh's descendants 2,1729
Shephatiah's descendants 37210
Arah's descendants 65211
Pahath-moab's descendants:
Jeshua's and Joab's descendants 2,81812
Elam's descendants 1,25413
Zattu's descendants 84514
 Zaccai's descendants 76015
Binnui's descendants 64816
Bebai's descendants 62817
Azgad's descendants 2,32218
Adonikam's descendants 66719

THIRD, LEARN

Today's reading begins with Nehemiah looking around at a mostly empty city—few people living in it, no houses built. As we noticed in an earlier email, building the wall required hundreds of builders. Where have they all gone? Why haven't they stayed to settle?

With the wall completed, God gives Nehemiah another task: Let's figure out who and where the people are.

Nehemiah makes a plan to gather all the Jews who currently live in Israel and create a registry. In planning for it, Nehemiah discovers a previously made registry, this one of the men and women who returned to Israel with Zerubbabel in the first wave of return from exile. Cue a long list of names and numbers.

Most interesting fact from the list (at least to me): the total number of people who returned from exile. "The whole combined assembly numbered 42,360 not including their 7,337 male and female servants, as well as their 245 male and female singers" (I love how, in light of their lack of a radio or Spotify, they just bring 245 singers along for the road trip).

Add up the singers and servants and everyone else and you get an influx of 49,942 people into the land of Israel. For comparison, That's 9,000 more people than live in Florence, AL. It's almost twice as many people as live in Troy, Ohio.

Now consider it in light of its historic context. At its height, the city of Babylon housed 200,000 people. If 49,942 people returned to Israel from exile in Babylon/Persia, that's 25% of the population.

I realized in this section of reading that the picture in my head has been WAY off. The entire time I've been imagining something like a western movie—dusty streets, outlaws starting brawls, a good sheriff inspiring the town to band together. The cast of characters was small— a couple hundred.

Nope.

42,000 Israelites+ returned from Babylon. It takes them more than 20 years to build a temple. 72 years after the temple's completion, it's still unprotected. Nehemiah shows up, and in 52 days a wall is erected and the problem's solved.

FOURTH, REFLECT

Why do you think Nehemiah is concerned about the genealogical record? What's God's purpose in gathering the people to be counted?

Does it matter that Jerusalem is mostly empty? Is there a reason to populate it?

I find it startling that 42,000 people couldn't build a wall until one man, strengthened by God, showed up. This morning I'm thinking about the power of a good leader and the unmistakable and unique gifting God gives to Nehemiah.

- Do you know leaders like that? What are the qualities they generally have?
- Is it possible God intends for you to be a leader like that? Where do you see a problem that needs to be fixed? What might you do to inspire the people around you to fix it?

FIFTH, LOOK

Where do you see God in today's passage?

We find plenty of lists like this in scripture. What's the point? What's God trying to communicate with all these names?

Don't forget your Week 3 teaching video!

WEEK 4

WEEK 4
Reading Guide

Monday	NEHEMIAH 8:1-8
Tuesday	NEHEMIAH 8:1-12
Wednesday	NEHEMIAH 8:13-18
Thursday	NEHEMIAH 8:1-18
Friday	NEHEMIAH 9:1-5

This week will include lots of re-reading. Totally worth it!

Day 1

FIRST, PRAY

God, open our eyes that we might see You in your Word.
Thank You for it. Make us hungry for it.

SECOND, READ

Nehemiah 8:1-8

All the people gathered together at the square in front of the Water Gate. They asked the scribe Ezra to bring the book of the law of Moses that the Lord had given Israel. On the first day of the seventh month, the priest Ezra brought the law before the assembly of men, women, and all who could listen with understanding. While he was facing the square in front of the Water Gate, he read out of it from daybreak until noon before the men, the women, and those who could understand. All the people listened attentively to the book of the law. The scribe Ezra stood on a high wooden platform made for this purpose. Mattithiah, Shema, Anaiah, Uriah, Hilkiah, and Maaseiah stood beside him on his right; to his left were Pedaiah, Mishael, Malchijah, Hashum, Hash-baddanah, Zechariah, and Meshullam. Ezra opened the book in full view of all the people, since he was elevated above everyone. As he opened it, all the people stood up. Ezra blessed the Lord, the great God, and with their hands uplifted all the people said, "Amen, Amen!" Then they knelt low and worshiped the Lord with their faces to the ground.
Jeshua, Bani, Sherebiah, Jamin, Akkub, Shabbethai, Hodiah, Maaseiah, Kelita, Azariah, Jozabad, Hanan, and Pelaiah, who were Levites, explained the law to the people as they stood in their places. They read out of the book of the law of God, translating and giving the meaning so that the people could understand what was read.

THIRD, LEARN

Whew. This chapter is packed with goodness. We'll re-read it (or most of it) three times this week, each day pointing out some new thing worth seeing.

To start today, let's try to get a sense of the scene:

We start off with "all the people gathered." What does "all the people" mean? Likely this means all the men and women who've come to Jerusalem for Nehemiah's census. If as many people live in Israel as did during the last count, we're talking about 50,000 folks—that's the same number of people it takes to fill Turner Field (former home of the Atlanta Braves) or roughly the number of people at a Taylor Swift concert.

It's a lot.

They meet up at the water gate, an entrance to the city possibly near the Gihon Spring (great metaphor—living water and all that jazz), definitely near the temple grounds and the courtyard.

Evidently they've asked for a reading of the law and the scribe Ezra has agreed. Who asked? "They" did. Perhaps the family patriarchs? Perhaps Nehemiah. We can't be sure. But what we do know is that the idea was warmly received by all the people of God. As Ezra read the law of Moses (from some kind of special stage designed for just this moment, and flanked by important dignitaries—don't miss how important this moment is to the Israelites), the people reacted like this:

1. They stood out of respect, lifted their hands in worship, and bowed in humility.
2. They welcomed Ezra's reading for six straight hours.
3. They listened "attentively."
4. They sought understanding, listening to explanation and translation.

Close your eyes and imagine an entire Taylor Swift concert rising to their feet as the Word of God is carried to the stage and opened. Imagine 100,000 raised hands, an army of voices yelling "Amen." Imagine every body dropping to the ground, bowed, slain in worship. And then one man's voice: *In the beginning God created the Heavens and the earth...*

FOURTH, REFLECT

Have you ever experienced something like this? A huge gathering of God's people, everyone devoted to hearing God's Word? How does it make you feel to be in a group like that?

Why do you think the Israelites are so hungry for the Law of Moses? What makes them so eager and attentive?

Do you think modern audiences would abide six hours of Bible reading? Why or why not?

Are you personally hungry for God's Word? Do you relate to the way the Israelites seem to venerate scripture? If not, why do you think that is? Consider praying and asking God to give you an appetite for His teaching.

We see in verses 7-8 a pack of roving Levites, working their way through the crowds explaining and translating, helping every listener understand the law. Translation probably looked more like paraphrasing than it did turning one language into another (though the Israelites had been in Babylon and Persia for a long time and may have been rusty at Hebrew). Three times in these eight verses we see a concentration on the importance of "understanding."

- What can we learn from this Levite practice of explanation? Why is it important? How might we mimic it in our gatherings?

- To say the Israelites listened to scripture in order to understand seems simple enough, BUT that's not always our goal when we read the Bible. Have you ever read for a reason other than understanding? Make a list of other possible reasons.

FIFTH, LOOK

Where do you see God in today's passage?

Where do the people of Israel see God in today's passage (be specific)? What's their reaction when they see Him? What does that reveal about Who they esteemed Him to be?

Day 2

FIRST, PRAY

God, open our eyes that we might see You in your Word.
Make us strong in your joy.

SECOND, READ

Nehemiah 8:1-12

All the people gathered together at the square in front of the Water Gate. They asked the scribe Ezra to bring the book of the law of Moses that the Lord had given Israel. On the first day of the seventh month, the priest Ezra brought the law before the assembly of men, women, and all who could listen with understanding. While he was facing the square in front of the Water Gate, he read out of it from daybreak until noon before the men, the women, and those who could understand. All the people listened attentively to the book of the law. The scribe Ezra stood on a high wooden platform made for this purpose.
Mattithiah, Shema, Anaiah, Uriah, Hilkiah, and Maaseiah stood beside him on his right; to his left were Pedaiah, Mishael, Malchijah, Hashum, Hash-baddanah, Zechariah, and Meshullam. Ezra opened the book in full view of all the people, since he was elevated above everyone. As he opened it, all the people stood up. Ezra blessed the Lord, the great God, and with their hands uplifted all the people said, "Amen, Amen!" Then they knelt low and worshiped the Lord with their faces to the ground.

Jeshua, Bani, Sherebiah, Jamin, Akkub, Shabbethai, Hodiah, Maaseiah, Kelita, Azariah, Jozabad, Hanan, and Pelaiah, who were Levites, explained the law to the people as they stood in their places. They read out of the book of the law of God, translating and giving the meaning so that the people could understand what was read.
Nehemiah the governor, Ezra the priest and scribe, and the Levites who were instructing the people said to all of them, "This day is holy to the Lord your God. Do

not mourn or weep." For all the people were weeping as they heard the words of the law. Then he said to them, "Go and eat what is rich, drink what is sweet, and send portions to those who have nothing prepared, since today is holy to our Lord. Do not grieve, because the joy of the Lord is your strength." And the Levites quieted all the people, saying, "Be still, since today is holy. Don't grieve." Then all the people began to eat and drink, send portions, and have a great celebration, because they had understood the words that were explained to them.

THIRD, LEARN

Today I want to take a minute and focus on this phrase: "The joy of the Lord is your strength." We print it on t-shirts and water bottles. We title conferences after it. But what does it mean?

Maybe for you it's simple, but for me, this phrase is complicated—so complicated I spent all day studying Hebrew words trying to understand it.

Here were my questions:

1. What is "joy"? Is it different that happiness?
2. Does "the joy of the Lord" mean joy that belongs to God—as in, when God is experiencing joy you are strong/because God is experiencing joy you are strong? Or does it mean the joy that comes from God—as in, the joy God gives you makes you strong?
3. What does "is your strength" mean? How does joy make a person strong?

Here are the answers (as best I can tell):

1. "Gladness," "joy," "rejoicing"—in Hebrew they're all the same word. The joy Nehemiah talks about here isn't different in type or essence from gladness or happiness; it's different in source. And just as the source of a wine (for example) determines the quality and complexity of the wine, the source of your joy determines its quality, depth, and sturdiness.

   Bottom line: It's NOT joy (or happiness or gladness or rejoicing) that brings us strength. It's "the joy of the Lord" that brings us strength. And that delineation is important. We ought not seek joy to find strength. We seek God and in finding God, find both joy and strength.

2. Is this God's joy or *our* joy we've received from God? We can't know. The original construction doesn't actually include the word "of." In Hebrew, the word joy and the word "the Lord" are crammed next to each other like this: "the joy the Lord" is your strength. After much consideration, I lean toward the first way of reading it: God's joy is your strength (more on that in the teaching video this week).

3. The word translated "strength" in this passage means, in Hebrew, "a fortified place." So, literally, Nehemiah, wall-builder, says, "The joy of the Lord is your fortified place, your walled city, your safe home." This changes the passage dramatically for me. Instead of seeing it as an injunction (joy makes you strong; be joyful and be strong), the phrase becomes a comfort (God's joy is a safe place). As I consider the context, this interpretation makes much more sense. The people of Israel are grieving and Nehemiah says "Don't grieve, for the joy of the Lord is your strength." He's not saying, "Buck up and get happy because God wants you to be joyful." He's saying, "God isn't mad at you. He's full of joy. You're safe in His joy."

FOURTH, REFLECT

Imagine you're an Israelite hearing these stories and commands for the very first time. How do you think you'd react? What would stick out to you?

Is this a happy story for the Israelites? (No yes or no answers accepted.) What about Israel's past complicates their relationship to the story?

Have you ever been in this position before: celebrating what you have but also grieving what you missed?

Do you sometimes let guilt get in the way of present joy? Write down an example. Why might that be a bad idea? How do we get past guilt and embrace joy? *Practical steps welcome.*

Do you feel safe in God's joy? Do you feel like you can safely come home to Him? Do you think of Him as a fortified place where you can belong and be protected? Write about a time when you came home and found Him welcoming you. Or write about a time when you came home to Him but didn't feel welcomed. Why do you think that was?

FIFTH, LOOK

Where do you see God in today's passage?

It's God's joy that makes us strong. What is God's joy?

What brings Him joy in this particular moment in Nehemiah?

How would you feel as a mother or father if you watched your children all come home from time away, gather in the family living room, and listen attentively to the family stories? Imagine it and write down three words to describe your emotions.

What does that teach you about who God is?

What's bringing God joy right now as He watches you?

Day 3

FIRST, PRAY

God, open our eyes that we might see You in your Word.
Teach us to celebrate.

SECOND, READ

Nehemiah 8:13-18

On the second day, the family heads of all the people, along with the priests and Levites, assembled before the scribe Ezra to study the words of the law. They found written in the law how the Lord had commanded through Moses that the Israelites should dwell in shelters during the festival of the seventh month. So they proclaimed and spread this news throughout their towns and in Jerusalem, saying, "Go out to the hill country and bring back branches of olive, wild olive, myrtle, palm, and other leafy trees to make shelters, just as it is written." The people went out, brought back branches, and made shelters for themselves on each of their rooftops and courtyards, the court of the house of God, the square by the Water Gate, and the square by the Ephraim Gate. The whole community that had returned from exile made shelters and lived in them. The Israelites had not celebrated like this from the days of Joshua son of Nun until that day. And there was tremendous joy. Ezra read out of the book of the law of God every day, from the first day to the last. The Israelites celebrated the festival for seven days, and on the eighth day there was a solemn assembly, according to the ordinance.

THIRD, LEARN

In verses 13:18 we find Israel returning to the Water Gate for day 2 of the public reading. Yesterday they spent the morning reading and the evening celebrating with good food and sweet drinks. Today, as they work their way through the Law, they read about a holiday celebration God commands His people to observe at exactly this time of year. What are the chances?! Rather than continuing the reading, the Israelites stop and give their attention to the commanded celebration.

You may know this prescribed holiday at Sukkoth or the Feast of Booths or the Feast of Tabernacles. It's a time to remember the wilderness wandering, the time when Israel didn't have homes made of stone or land to cultivate. This is the holiday on which Israel celebrates God's provision in the wilderness.

Could this be more perfect? Yesterday Israel came face to face with their own sin and grief over being exiled from God's presence and failing to follow His laws. They saw themselves in the wandering Jews, scared to take the promised land. Today, they're reminded that even in the exile, even in their disobedience, God was with them, providing temporary shelter until they could finally come home to something better.

So the Israelites collect branches and make huts and camp out with their families inside the city walls, like children building forts in the living room. If you'd seen the city from the air at night, you'd have seen thousands of tiny campfires, flaming polka dots. And around every one of those fires you'd have found families, faces aglow, giving thanks for God's provision in the wilderness.

In verse 17 we read, "From the days of Joshua son of Nun until that day, the Israelites had not celebrated it like this. And their joy was very great."

This is the best Feast of Booths in the history of Feasts of Booths. If their joy was very great, can you even imagine God's?

FOURTH, REFLECT

I am a huge fan of the holy celebration. I see Israel here piling up sticks into ten thousand tiny forts, and I see God engineering moments of partnership, spectacle, and delight. The little tasks of our celebrations (traditional foods, repeated stories, specific colors and smells, characters, songs) are the cells and atoms of our joy.

Why do celebrations matter?

1. They enable us to share in God's joy and in sharing that joy, to be made strong and secure. God's joy reminds us we belong. It reminds us we're safe.
2. They help us remember. Celebrations, with all of their cues (smells, tastes, sounds, even temperatures) trigger our deepest, happiest memories. Holidays become packed with year after year of shared joys and shared stories.
3. They connect us to one another. When do you see family you haven't seen in ages? At the holidays. And when you get in your car to leave, feeling happy and rooted, you wonder why it is you never call your cousin.

These days almost all our holidays are completely secular in nature. We rarely throw a holy party. And that, friends, is a failure. God packs the Old Testament with required celebrations, celebrations like meals packed into the rhythm of daily life, sustaining His people, keeping them close—to Him and to each other.

In the New Testament we don't find these kinds of seasonal celebrations—not exactly. Instead we find Christians who're meeting together EVERY DAY, sharing meals, learning together, singing together, and praying together.

We also can't miss that the first communion happens in the context of a holiday celebration (Passover) and ought to be, for us, the most powerful of all celebrations, enabling us to share in God's joy, helping us remember, and connecting us to one another.

Bottom line: We need to celebrate more. We need to take time to bask in the Lord's joy, to feast and sing and tell stories and build ridiculous palm tree forts in the middle of the living room.

- Do you feel like celebration is a part of your experience as a follower of God? If so, give an example. If not, why not?

What might it look like for you to celebrate God's work in your life? Imagine/plan a recurring party that would meet the three qualifications of holy celebration (God's-joy-sharing, memory-jogging, & connecting).

FIFTH, LOOK.

Where do you see God in today's passage?

How do you think God reacts to the festivities? How does the celebration make Him feel?

Why do you think God commanded Israel to observe this holiday?

Day 4

FIRST, PRAY

God, open our eyes that we might see You in your Word.
Empower us to see and live Your story.

SECOND, READ

Nehemiah 8:1-18

All the people gathered together at the square in front of the Water Gate. They asked the scribe Ezra to bring the book of the law of Moses that the Lord had given Israel. On the first day of the seventh month, the priest Ezra brought the law before the assembly of men, women, and all who could listen with understanding. While he was facing the square in front of the Water Gate, he read out of it from daybreak until noon before the men, the women, and those who could understand. All the people listened attentively to the book of the law. The scribe Ezra stood on a high wooden platform made for this purpose. Mattithiah, Shema, Anaiah, Uriah, Hilkiah, and Maaseiah stood beside him on his right; to his left were Pedaiah, Mishael, Malchijah, Hashum, Hash-baddanah, Zechariah, and Meshullam. Ezra opened the book in full view of all the people, since he was elevated above everyone. As he opened it, all the people stood up. Ezra blessed the Lord, the great God, and with their hands uplifted all the people said, "Amen, Amen!" Then they knelt low and worshiped the Lord with their faces to the ground.

Jeshua, Bani, Sherebiah, Jamin, Akkub, Shabbethai, Hodiah, Maaseiah, Kelita, Azariah, Jozabad, Hanan, and Pelaiah, who were Levites, explained the law to the people as they stood in their places. They read out of the book of the law of God, translating and giving the meaning so that the people could understand what was read. Nehemiah the governor, Ezra the priest and scribe, and the Levites who were instructing the people said to all of them, "This day is holy to the Lord your God. Do not mourn or weep."

For all the people were weeping as they heard the words of the law. Then he said to them, "Go and eat what is rich, drink what is sweet, and send portions to those who have nothing prepared, since today is holy to our Lord. Do not grieve, because the joy of the Lord is your strength." And the Levites quieted all the people, saying, "Be still, since today is holy. Don't grieve." Then all the people began to eat and drink, send portions, and have a great celebration, because they had understood the words that were explained to them.

On the second day, the family heads of all the people, along with the priests and Levites, assembled before the scribe Ezra to study the words of the law. They found written in the law how the Lord had commanded through Moses that the Israelites should dwell in shelters during the festival of the seventh month. So they proclaimed and spread this news throughout their towns and in Jerusalem, saying, "Go out to the hill country and bring back branches of olive, wild olive, myrtle, palm, and other leafy trees to make shelters, just as it is written." The people went out, brought back branches, and made shelters for themselves on each of their rooftops and courtyards, the court of the house of God, the square by the Water Gate, and the square by the Ephraim Gate. The whole community that had returned from exile made shelters and lived in them. The Israelites had not celebrated like this from the days of Joshua son of Nun until that day. And there was tremendous joy. Ezra read out of the book of the law of God every day, from the first day to the last. The Israelites celebrated the festival for seven days, and on the eighth day there was a solemn assembly, according to the ordinance.

THIRD, LEARN

We're reading this passage one more time, this time altogether, to take one more look at the Israelites' reaction to the Word of God. We've said they responded with respect and eagerness. We noted how powerfully the Word convicted them of their own guilt, leading them to grieve. And we noted how quick they were to put the Law into action by celebrating the Feast of Booths.

Question: Why do the Israelites feel so connected to this book?

Why are they so hungry to hear it read? Why are they so moved? Why are they so eager to put it into action?

My best guess: Because it's their story.

For these men and women, the words being read aren't some long ago history. They're not "Once upon a time." This story is their story. This God is their God. This land is their land. The characters are their ancestors, and even now they may have a sense that they are, in this moment, living scripture.

Ezra, standing up there on podium—he's a direct descendant of Aaron, the very first high priest. Ezra is reading stories about his great, great, great, great, great... grandfather. Ezra probably looks like Aaron, the same Palestinian sun on his cheeks, the same smell of animal and oil on his shirt, the same concentration-ploughed furrows in his brow.

The men and women in the crowd are descendants of Judah, of Joshua, Rahab, and King David. They are the children of promise, the stars in Abraham's inky wide sky. They cannot listen disinterestedly.

FOURTH, REFLECT

My great, great, great (etc.) grandfather was not Aaron or David or even some minor character like maybe "third magician in Pharoah's court." The stories in the Bible aren't my family's history—not like they are for Ezra or Nehemiah. I don't think of Jerusalem as my homeland. I don't even keep the Law of Moses.

And at the same time, these stories are totally my stories and totally my history. The STORY (the all caps story) of God's relationship with mankind, IS our story. In it, we find our identity and our destiny.

Recently I heard Russell Moore give a lecture on why Christians should read more fiction. He said that people who understand stories (particularly plot) are the people who understand God's activity in the universe. I nodded my head so hard I got a crick in my neck.

Part of what's happening in Nehemiah 8 is that Israel is finding her place in the story. These men and women are figuring out who they are (villains? heroes? love interest?

knight? captured princess? dragon?) and where they are along the arch of the plot.

They devote themselves to the Word of God, because the story of scripture is the story of their lives, and understanding the story of scripture is the only way to understand God's work in their lives.

For seven days the Israelites devote themselves to the story—because they *have to know* how it ends, because they'll be called upon to live an ending themselves.

It's the same for us. We can't understand God without understanding His story. We can't relate to Him properly without knowing how He's related to men and women throughout history.

Every day you are entering a story, the story of God's love for humankind, and in order to inhabit that story, you need to understand it. You need to know what kind of character you are. You need to know what kind of character God is. And you need to have a sense of how the story plays out.

- Do you feel like you're living a story? How might thinking of yourself inside the grand story of scripture and God's work in the universe shape the way you live?

- What kind of ending are you expecting for your story? What do you need to do in order to live toward that ending?

- If scripture has a recurring plot, what would you say it is? What cycle do humans find themselves in as they relate to God?

- What would you say is the theme of God's Word?

FIFTH, LOOK

Where do you see God in today's passage?

What do the Israelites learn about God as they perceive His character in the story of human history? What kind of character is He?

How does the way you feel about God's character shape the way you interact with Him? How does it shape the story you're living?

Day 5

FIRST, PRAY

God, open our eyes that we might see You in your Word.
Empower us to repent.

SECOND, READ

Nehemiah 9:1-5

> On the twenty-fourth day of this month the Israelites assembled; they were fasting, wearing sackcloth, and had put dust on their heads. Those of Israelite descent separated themselves from all foreigners, and they stood and confessed their sins and the iniquities of their ancestors. While they stood in their places, they read from the book of the law of the Lord their God for a fourth of the day and spent another fourth of the day in confession and worship of the Lord their God. Jeshua, Bani, Kadmiel, Shebaniah, Bunni, Sherebiah, Bani, and Chenani stood on the raised platform built for the Levites and cried out loudly to the Lord their God. Then the Levites—Jeshua, Kadmiel, Bani, Hashabneiah, Sherebiah, Hodiah, Shebaniah, and Pethahiah—said, "Stand up. Blessed be the Lord your God from everlasting to everlasting." Blessed be your glorious name, and may it be exalted above all blessing and praise.

THIRD, LEARN

The celebration is over, and it's time to attend to that guilt. What do the people of Israel do?

- They mark themselves with signs of grief and repentance—sackcloth and dust. Sackcloth was a coarse material usually made of black goat's hair. It's an uncomfortable outer symbol of inner discomfort. The ashes are similar—a sign of humility and a recognition of uncleanness.

- They separate themselves from foreigners. As they read the Law of Moses, Israel realizes they've become much too intertwined with the cultures around them, intermarrying, participating in pagan religious practices, etc. Repentance demands they cut those ties.
- They confess their sins and the sins of their ancestors.
- They worship God.

FOURTH, REFLECT

When you read scripture and find yourself face to face with your own failings and guilt, how do you respond? Think through the last time you found yourself convicted. How did you react?

When you know you need to repent, are you quick to cut ties with those who would pull you back into sin? Or do you struggle to end relationships (even destructive ones)? Why is it so important to get away from those influences?

Is it possible to repent without putting down the sin you're repenting of? Have you ever tried to repent but couldn't quit your sin? Why do you think it was hard to leave it behind?

Have you ever participated in public confession? How did it make you feel? Why is this an important step in the process of repentance?

What do you think is the point of confessing the sins of your ancestors? Is this something that might make sense for you to do? Do you see strong patterns of sin in your family history? What benefit might there be to acknowledging those?

I don't know about you, but for me, some of my most powerful moments of worship to God have come on the heels of confession. I can think of a few reasons why that might be true:

1. You're not distracted from God's goodness by your own lack of goodness. Sin makes us self-aware. When we confess, we take our eyes off ourselves and look back at God.
2. You feel unburdened. That lightness and freedom so often leads to reckless, eager worship.
3. You and God have cleared the air. You're not trying to hide something from God. You're not worried God's mad at you. There is nothing standing between you and Him, which means you can draw oh-so-near to him.
4. You've been brought into deeper relationship with God through the act of vulnerability and dependance. Side note: This works with humans, too. Every time you confess a sin against a friend *to* that friend. Your vulnerability and their grace will knit you two together.
5. You're grateful. After confession we receive the gift of forgiveness—a gift so big and so generous we can't help but praise the Giver.

If you have something you need to confess, DO IT. Confession isn't something to fear. It's a gift, an opportunity to grow more deeply in love with God and an open door to worship.

FIFTH, LOOK

Where do you see God in today's passage?

How do you think God responds to Israel's repentance?

THIS WEEK'S TEACHING VIDEO HAS ME CRYING. DON'T MISS OUT! (JLGERHARDT.COM/FRESHSTART)

WEEK 5

WEEK 5
Reading Guide

Monday	NEHEMIAH 9:6-21
Tuesday	NEHEMIAH 9:22-31
Wednesday	NEHEMIAH 9:32-10:29
Thursday	NEHEMIAH 10:30-39
Friday	NEHEMIAH 11:1-12:26

Day 1

FIRST, PRAY

God, open our eyes that we might see You in your Word.
Help us know You and remember You.

SECOND, READ

Nehemiah 9:6-21

> You, Lord, are the only God.
> You created the heavens,
> the highest heavens with all their stars,
> the earth and all that is on it,
> the seas and all that is in them.
> You give life to all of them,
> and all the stars of heaven worship you.
> You, the Lord, are the God who chose Abram
> and brought him out of Ur of the Chaldeans,
> and changed his name to Abraham.
> You found his heart faithful in your sight,
> and made a covenant with him
> to give the land of the Canaanites,
> Hethites, Amorites, Perizzites,
> Jebusites, and Girgashites—
> to give it to his descendants.
> You have fulfilled your promise,
> for you are righteous.
> You saw the oppression of our ancestors in Egypt
> and heard their cry at the Red Sea.
> You performed signs and wonders against Pharaoh,

all his officials, and all the people of his land,

for you knew how arrogantly they treated our ancestors.

You made a name for yourself

that endures to this day.

You divided the sea before them,

and they crossed through it on dry ground.

You hurled their pursuers into the depths

like a stone into raging water.

You led them with a pillar of cloud by day,

and with a pillar of fire by night,

to illuminate the way they should go.

You came down on Mount Sinai,

and spoke to them from heaven.

You gave them impartial ordinances, reliable instructions,

and good statutes and commands.

You revealed your holy Sabbath to them,

and gave them commands, statutes, and instruction

through your servant Moses.

You provided bread from heaven for their hunger;

you brought them water from the rock for their thirst.

You told them to go in and possess the land

you had sworn to give them.

But our ancestors acted arrogantly;

they became stiff-necked and did not listen to your commands.

They refused to listen

and did not remember your wonders

you performed among them.

They became stiff-necked and appointed a leader

to return to their slavery in Egypt.

But you are a forgiving God,

gracious and compassionate,

slow to anger and abounding in faithful love,

and you did not abandon them.

Even after they had cast an image of a calf

for themselves and said,

"This is your god who brought you out of Egypt,"

and they had committed terrible blasphemies,
you did not abandon them in the wilderness
because of your great compassion.
During the day the pillar of cloud
never turned away from them,
guiding them on their journey.
And during the night the pillar of fire
illuminated the way they should go.
You sent your good Spirit to instruct them.
You did not withhold your manna from their mouths,
and you gave them water for their thirst.
You provided for them in the wilderness forty years,
and they lacked nothing.
Their clothes did not wear out,
and their feet did not swell.

THIRD, LEARN

We ended last week's reading with Israel's communal repentance and confession. We begin this week with the prayer of praise (possibly a song) they pray during that confessional gathering.

It begins as a recap of everything they've learned about God's character, activity, and identity during their seven days of Bible reading, working from Genesis all the way through the books of history until the present moment.

Take a moment and underline or highlight every phrase that starts "You _____." By my count you'll find 30 in today's reading.

FOURTH, LOOK

Reflect on these 30 "You" statements. Where do you see God in today's passage?

Who is God according to this prayer? What has He done for His people? What has He promised to do for His people?

What does God's past faithfulness mean to you personally? What can you expect from God based on this passage of scripture?

FIFTH, REFLECT

- If you were to write a prayer like this, which moments in God's history with His people would you include? Which stories are the most powerful reminders for you of His love, compassion, and faithfulness?

- What moments from your family's history might you include? Which moments from your own life?

This isn't simply a prayer of praise. It's also a prayer of confession. Israel says "But they, our ancestors, became arrogant and stiff-necked, and they did not obey your commands."

- What has Israel learned from the behavior of those who came before them?

Day 2

FIRST, PRAY

God, open our eyes that we might see You in your Word.
Remind us that You're not like us.

SECOND, READ

Nehemiah 9:22-31

> You gave them kingdoms and peoples
> and established boundaries for them.
> They took possession
> of the land of King Sihon of Heshbon
> and of the land of King Og of Bashan.
> You multiplied their descendants
> like the stars of the sky
> and brought them to the land
> you told their ancestors to go in and possess.
> So their descendants went in and possessed the land:
> You subdued the Canaanites who inhabited the land before them
> and handed their kings and the surrounding peoples over to them,
> to do as they pleased with them.
> They captured fortified cities and fertile land
> and took possession of well-supplied houses,
> cisterns cut out of rock, vineyards,
> olive groves, and fruit trees in abundance.
> They ate, were filled,
> became prosperous, and delighted in your great goodness.
> But they were disobedient and rebelled against you.
> They flung your law behind their backs

and killed your prophets
who warned them
in order to turn them back to you.
They committed terrible blasphemies.
So you handed them over to their enemies,
who oppressed them.
In their time of distress, they cried out to you,
and you heard from heaven.
In your abundant compassion
you gave them deliverers, who rescued them
from the power of their enemies.
But as soon as they had relief,
they again did what was evil in your sight.
So you abandoned them to the power of their enemies,
who dominated them.
When they cried out to you again,
you heard from heaven and rescued them
many times in your compassion.
You warned them to turn back to your law,
but they acted arrogantly
and would not obey your commands.
They sinned against your ordinances,
which a person will live by if he does them.
They stubbornly resisted, stiffened their necks,
and would not obey.
You were patient with them for many years,
and your Spirit warned them through your prophets,
but they would not listen.
Therefore, you handed them over to the surrounding peoples.
However, in your abundant compassion,
you did not destroy them or abandon them,
for you are a gracious and compassionate God.

THIRD, LEARN

As this prayer builds we find the speaker alternating back and forth between "You" (God) and "they" (Israel), resulting in a kind of dance between God and His people. They're joined through God's attention and love, and they're pushed apart by Israel's disobedience. Together, apart, together, apart...

Part of what's achieved in these verses is a contrast between God's character and Israel's character. God is not like Israel, and Israel is not like God. This is a powerful thing to remember as we relate to God: He is NOT like us. He's generous when we're greedy. He's patient when we're impatient. He's merciful when we're cruel. He loves us when we hate Him.

If we're not careful, we'll project our own human failings onto our Father. We'll decide He's angry because we'd be angry if we were Him. We'll decide He's abandoned us, because our father abandoned us. We'll decide He doesn't love us, because our husband doesn't seem to love us. We'll assume He can't do anything to fix a situation, because we can't do anything to fix a situation.

Nehemiah 9 and the Law of Moses it summarizes teach us that God is not like us. *And that's great news.*

FOURTH, LOOK

Where do you see God in today's passage?

Just like yesterday, take a moment and look for the "You" statements. What do we learn about God in today's reading? Really dig in here. Who is He?

If this is all you do today, it will have been a good day.

Each revelation about God's faithful love builds upon the revelation before it. How does this fast-paced, very long list of God's loving acts make you feel about God? What does the form of the prayer/song/poem achieve?

FIFTH, REFLECT

Take a moment as you end your study time today to reflect specifically on God's compassion. The Israelites pray here (about their ancestors), "In your compassion you delivered them time after time" (NIV rendering of verse 28).

- Has God delivered you time after time? Think of a specific example or two.
- Do you truly believe God will deliver you time after time? Be completely honest.
- Do you sometimes feel like maybe God's compassion will run out? If so, talk to God about it. Pray telling God how you feel, asking Him to help you trust his mercy.
- Consider writing the words "time after time" in Sharpie on your forearm (or, if temporary Sharpie tattoos aren't your thing, write it on an index card and put it somewhere you'll see it). See how those words affect you as you catch glimpses of them throughout the day.

Day 3

FIRST, PRAY

God, open our eyes that we might see You in your Word.
Have mercy on us, and free us from the slavery we deserve.

SECOND, READ

Nehemiah 9:32-10:29

> So now, our God—the great, mighty,and awe-inspiring God who keeps his gracious
> covenant—do not view lightly all the hardships that have afflicted us,
> our kings and leaders,
> our priests and prophets,
> our ancestors and all your people,
> from the days of the Assyrian kings until today.
> You are righteous concerning all that has happened to us,
> because you have acted faithfully,
> while we have acted wickedly.
> Our kings, leaders, priests, and ancestors
> did not obey your law
> or listen to your commands
> and warnings you gave them.
> When they were in their kingdom,
> with your abundant goodness that you gave them,
> and in the spacious and fertile land you set before them,
> they would not serve you or turn from their wicked ways.
> Here we are today,
> slaves in the land you gave our ancestors
> so that they could enjoy its fruit and its goodness.
> Here we are—slaves in it!

Its abundant harvest goes to the kings
you have set over us,
because of our sins.
They rule over our bodies
and our livestock as they please.
We are in great distress.
In view of all this, we are making a binding agreement in writing on a sealed document containing the names of our leaders, Levites, and priests.

[Insert long list of names, 10:1-27]

The rest of the people—the priests, Levites, gatekeepers, singers, and temple servants, along with their wives, sons, and daughters, everyone who is able to understand and who has separated themselves from the surrounding peoples to obey the law of God—join with their noble brothers and commit themselves with a sworn oath to follow the law of God given through God's servant Moses and to obey carefully all the commands, ordinances, and statutes of the Lord our Lord.

THIRD, LEARN

This is the end of the prayer, a prayer rooted in worship and wet with guilt. Verses 32-35 are more of what we've seen so far. God is mighty and awesome, loving. Israel is disobedient. Verse 33 sums it up well: "You have acted faithfully, while we acted wickedly."

In verse 36, however, we sense a shift, a new element being introduced—a differentiation between past Israel and current Israel beginning with the words, "Here we are today" and then, "Here we are—slaves."

Did you remember the Israelites were slaves? I'd completely forgotten.

I see Nehemiah acting with power and wealth and authority, and I forget that ultimately he answers to Assyria. I see the Jews settling their land, rebuilding, farming, and I imagine they've been liberated from their shackles. How could people with this much opportunity and volition be slaves?

This oversight on my part comes from a misunderstanding of slavery in the ancient world. Slavery in Persia in the fifth century looked very little like American slavery in the 1800s. In Babylon, for example, slaves were educated, trained, and housed and dressed as members of the family. Slaves could and often did give testimony in court. Slaves could start businesses. Slaves could buy their freedom. Slaves had rights under the law including prohibitions against violence and the right to be kept in the same home as their spouses and children.

In this moment, the Israelites have been charged by the nation of Assyria to return to Jerusalem and make it a profitable territory. Yes, they build the walls and farm the land, but the walls and the land don't belong to them. They belong to Assyria.

Interestingly, Nehemiah here is both slave and agent of the master. His job is to make sure the Israelites stay in line and do the work—for the benefit of Assyria's coffers.

What are the practical difficulties of Israel's slavery? A lack of wealth due to heavy taxation, no feeling of ownership or personal responsibility for the nation, lack of national identity, inability to chart a course for the future...

There's a lot about slavery that's hard. Israel prays, "We are in great distress."

Why is Israel in this position? Verse 37 provides an answer: "Because of our sins."

What we need to catch here is that Israel owns the guilt that resulted in their slavery. They look at their situation, evaluate their behavior (and the behavior of their ancestors), and recognize both cause and effect. This prayer is one giant, "Our bad."

And as soon as the prayer closes, Israel gets busy correcting their mistakes...

FOURTH, REFLECT

- Are you a slave to anything? Does anything have power over you? How did you end up in slavery?

- How good are you at owning your guilt? How quick are you to admit your mistakes?

- In a tough situation or trying circumstance do you usually evaluate your own guilt or innocence to see whether or not you're experiencing the consequences of sin? What does that process look like? Who might you involve as a second voice of wisdom?

Slavery isn't new for the Israelites—in fact, the nation of Israel was forged in slavery in Egypt. After this moment in Nehemiah, Israel will be enslaved again by the Greeks and, in a couple hundred years, by the Romans. When Jesus comes, he preaches freedom to a nation of (essentially) slaves.

In John 8:32 Jesus says to the Israelites, "You will know the truth, and the truth will set you free."

Surely, after roughly 600 years of slavery, this would be a most appealing promise. It's what the Jews here in Nehemiah desire most. But, in a fascinating turn, the Jews in Jesus' audience respond, "We are Abraham's descendants and have never been slaves of anyone. How can you say that we shall be set free?"

Wait a minute. *What?*

This reaction is the exact opposite of the reaction we find in Nehemiah 9. In Nehemiah the people hear the truth of scripture and respond with humble recognition and apology. In John, the Israelites hear the truth of Jesus and respond with arrogant deceit. They're completely unable to see themselves clearly. They've put their fingers in their ears and la, la, la-ed their way into a false sense of superiority and moral righteousness.

FIFTH, LOOK

Where do you see God in today's passage?

In verse 33 we read, "You are righteous concerning all that has happened to us, because you have acted faithfully, while we have acted wickedly."

- Have you ever experienced God's righteousness and faithful love even when you yourself were acting wickedly? Consider an example.

- How has God been faithful to you? *How has God been faithful to you this week?*

Day 4

FIRST, PRAY

God, open our eyes that we might see You in your Word.
We devote ourselves to your commands.

SECOND, READ

Nehemiah 10:30-39

We will not give our daughters in marriage to the surrounding peoples and will not take their daughters as wives for our sons.

When the surrounding peoples bring merchandise or any kind of grain to sell on the Sabbath day, we will not buy from them on the Sabbath or a holy day. We will also leave the land uncultivated in the seventh year and will cancel every debt.

We will impose the following commands on ourselves:

To give an eighth of an ounce of silver yearly for the service of the house of our God: the bread displayed before the Lord, the daily grain offering, the regular burnt offering, the Sabbath and New Moon offerings, the appointed festivals, the holy things, the sin offerings to atone for Israel, and for all the work of the house of our God.

We have cast lots among the priests, Levites, and people for the donation of wood by our ancestral families at the appointed times each year. They are to bring the wood to our God's house to burn on the altar of the Lord our God, as it is written in the law.

We will bring the firstfruits of our land and of every fruit tree to the Lord's house year by year. We will also bring the firstborn of our sons and our livestock, as prescribed by the law, and will bring the firstborn of our herds and flocks to the house of our God, to the priests who serve in our God's house. We will bring a loaf from our first batch of dough to the priests at the storerooms of the house of our God. We will also bring the firstfruits of our grain offerings, of every fruit tree, and of the new wine and fresh oil. A tenth of our land's produce belongs to the Levites, for the Levites are to collect the one-tenth offering in all our agricultural towns. A priest from Aaron's descendants is to accompany the

Levites when they collect the tenth, and the Levites are to take a tenth of this offering to the storerooms of the treasury in the house of our God. For the Israelites and the Levites are to bring the contributions of grain, new wine, and fresh oil to the storerooms where the articles of the sanctuary are kept and where the priests who minister are, along with the gatekeepers and singers. We will not neglect the house of our God.

THIRD, LEARN

What do we make of Israel's oath?

Clearly it comes from a humble heart and an eager desire to follow the Law of Moses. All of these promises are simply commands God has asked His people to keep. Consider this moment like a vow renewal ceremony. The bride and groom have grown apart, the bride has been unfaithful, but now she's recommitting herself to those same promises she made years ago.

It's lovely.

It may be the Law of Moses itself that inspires the idea of making an oath. Search the word "oath" in the book of Genesis and you'll find it appears 14 times (18 in the book of Deuteronomy). God makes oaths to Israel, and Israel makes oaths to God. This is yet another oath in a long history of oaths.

As beautiful as this moment seems, it definitely makes me squirm. It reminds me of moments when my own children have made oaths they've promptly broken. Or of moments when my husband made promises (or I made promises) we both knew we wouldn't keep.

There's something sacred about the optimism (hope?), but there's also something very sad about knowing, even as the oath is slipping from their lips, that some among them have no intention of doing what it takes to keep their promise.

Should we promise anyway? Isn't aspiring worthwhile?

Here's what Jesus will say in a few hundred years:

> "Again, you have heard that it was said to the people long ago, 'Do not break your oath, but fulfill to the Lord the vows you have made.' But I tell you, do not swear an oath at all: either by heaven, for it is God's throne; or by the earth, for it is his footstool; or by Jerusalem, for it is the city of the Great King. And do not swear by your head, for you cannot make even one hair white or black. All you need to say is simply 'Yes' or 'No'; anything beyond this comes from the evil one."

What's Jesus saying? I think the gist is this: stop making fancy promises with a hundred signatures and flowery language. Just say yes to God (or no if that's the honest answer) and get to it.

I expect Jesus may very well have this exact oath in mind as he speaks, knowing Israel failed at keeping it, and wishing so deeply that Israel might have been spared the emotional crash of failing so quickly.

FOURTH, REFLECT

How good are you at keeping promises? What's the problem with making promises we don't keep?

Are you a yes or no kind of person or are you a flowery, pinkie promise, I-swear-on-my mother's-grave kind of person? What might be the problem with so much build up surrounding our oaths?

Why do you think Jesus forbids oaths?

Have you ever had someone make you a promise you wish they hadn't made? How did it feel when they broke their promise? Take a moment to imagine how God feels in this moment with Israel, once again promising to keep the Law.

FIFTH, LOOK

Where do you see God in today's passage?

Here's a challenging question (I have no idea what the right answer might be):

- How do you think God feels about the "binding agreement" Israel makes here?
- Make a list of reasons God might approve of the agreement and a list of reasons God might not like it.

Day 5

FIRST, PRAY

God, open our eyes that we might see You in your Word.
Write our names on Your list.

SECOND, READ

Nehemiah 11:1-12:26 (11:1-9 and 12:22-26 included below)

Now the leaders of the people stayed in Jerusalem, and the rest of the people cast lots for one out of ten to come and live in Jerusalem, the holy city, while the other nine-tenths remained in their towns. The people blessed all the men who volunteered to live in Jerusalem.

These are the heads of the province who stayed in Jerusalem (but in the villages of Judah each lived on his own property in their towns—the Israelites, priests, Levites, temple servants, and descendants of Solomon's servants—while some of the descendants of Judah and Benjamin settled in Jerusalem):

Judah's descendants:
Athaiah son of Uzziah, son of Zechariah, son of Amariah, son of Shephatiah, son of Mahalalel, of Perez's descendants; and Maaseiah son of Baruch, son of Col-hozeh, son of Hazaiah, son of Adaiah, son of Joiarib, son of Zechariah, a descendant of the Shilonite. The total number of Perez's descendants, who settled in Jerusalem, was 468 capable men.
These were Benjamin's descendants:
Sallu son of Meshullam, son of Joed, son of Pedaiah, son of Kolaiah, son of Maaseiah, son of Ithiel, son of Jeshaiah, and after him Gabbai and Sallai: 928. Joel son of Zichri was the officer over them, and Judah son of Hassenuah was second in command over the city [...]

In the days of Eliashib, Joiada, Johanan, and Jaddua, the heads of the families of the Levites and priests were recorded while Darius the Persian ruled. Levi's descendants, the family heads, were recorded in the Book of the Historical Events during the days of Johanan son of Eliashib. The heads of the Levites—Hashabiah, Sherebiah, and Jeshua son of Kadmiel, along with their relatives opposite them—gave praise and thanks, division by division, as David the man of God had prescribed. This included Mattaniah, Bakbukiah, and Obadiah. Meshullam, Talmon, and Akkub were gatekeepers who guarded the storerooms at the city gates. These served in the days of Joiakim son of Jeshua, son of Jozadak, and in the days of Nehemiah the governor and Ezra the priest and scribe.

THIRD, LEARN

Over 3,000 men stay in Jerusalem after the prayer of confession and praise.

Why is it important for a large number of Israelites to settle in Jerusalem? Why can't they just go back to their homes? If Jerusalem is to be a symbolic seat of power it needs to actually be powerful. With a tiny population, Jerusalem is vulnerable to attack.

Fun fact: Because of the process used to recruit people to Jerusalem (lots), the citizens end up being pretty diverse (from a few different tribes, not all family). That's city life—people who're different from each other learning how to be united.

Today's reading is undeniably boring. It's a long list of names we don't know and can't pronounce. Still, it's worth a moment of our attention. These lists in chapters 11 and 12 follow in the tradition of similar lists from the book of Numbers. In Numbers, God records the names of the nation-founders, the ones who escaped from Egypt, survived the wilderness wandering, and prepared for settlement in Israel. Here, we again find a list of nation-founders, men like seeds, planted with the purpose of a rich later harvest. Keeping track of their names is like writing down the names of the men and women who first came to the new world. They're doing something historic; write it down! Remember!

Also important about these lists: Because God kept track of Israel's descendants in scripture, we're able to trace the lineage of Christ. God made a promise to send Jesus via David and Jessie and Abraham, and we need records to verify that He kept His promise. Thus, throughout Israel's history, God has been fastidious about genealogy.

FOURTH, REFLECT

Huge props to the leaders of Israel who all agree to settle in Jerusalem! It's a sacrifice to be away from the land and the promise of agricultural wealth, a sacrifice the leaders make as an example to those who'll be chosen by lot (like kings leading the charge into battle or captains going down with the ship).

Sometimes it feels lonely to follow God and do what's right. Lists like these lists (full of thousands of God's people, all on mission) remind us we're not alone.

Take a minute today to make a long list of people you're serving God alongside. Who are your partners in Kingdom work? When you're done with the list, pray over it.

If you're anything like me, you might be wondering, "Where are the women in these lists?" Why doesn't God record their names? Aren't they important?

I could give you information about the standing and treatment of women in this time period, perhaps even argue that God goes above and beyond cultural expectations in including the daughters who worked on the wall in an earlier list. But ultimately, God is capable of overturning or upending cultural expectations should He want to, and so we have to assume He didn't want to. Not yet.

- How does that make you feel? If it's uncomfortable, be sure to talk to God about it one-on-one.
- Consider another list, this one in Matthew chapter 1. What's different about this list?Does seeing women's names in one of these lists make you feel better? Why or why not?

FIFTH, LOOK

Where do you see God in today's passage?

Why do you think God includes so many lists of names in scripture? What does it say about Who God is that He values lists like this?

Is God currently keeping a list of names (Revelation 3:5)? Whose name makes the list?

IN THIS WEEK'S TEACHING VIDEO WE ZOOM IN ON ONE IMPORTANT
TRUTH: GOD IS NOT LIKE YOU. CHECK IT OUT AT
JLGERHARDT.COM/FRESHSTART.

WEEK 6

WEEK 6
Reading Guide

Monday	NEHEMIAH 12:27-43
Tuesday	NEHEMIAH 12:27-47
Wednesday	NEHEMIAH 13:1-30
Thursday	NEHEMIAH 13:1-30
Friday	NEHEMIAH 13:10-30

Lots of re-reading this week; Embrace the chance to take a second look.

Day 1

FIRST, PRAY

God, open our eyes that we might see You in your Word.
Give us hearts that ache for celebration.

SECOND, READ

Nehemiah 12:27-43

At the dedication of the wall of Jerusalem, they sent for the Levites wherever they lived and brought them to Jerusalem to celebrate the joyous dedication with thanksgiving and singing accompanied by cymbals, harps, and lyres. The singers gathered from the region around Jerusalem, from the settlements of the Netophathites, from Beth-gilgal, and from the fields of Geba and Azmaveth, for they had built settlements for themselves around Jerusalem. After the priests and Levites had purified themselves, they purified the people, the city gates, and the wall.

Then I brought the leaders of Judah up on top of the wall, and I appointed two large processions that gave thanks. One went to the right on the wall, toward the Dung Gate. Hoshaiah and half the leaders of Judah followed, along with Azariah, Ezra, Meshullam, Judah, Benjamin, Shemaiah, Jeremiah, and some of the priests' sons with trumpets, and Zechariah son of Jonathan, son of Shemaiah, son of Mattaniah, son of Micaiah, son of Zaccur, son of Asaph followed as well as his relatives—Shemaiah, Azarel, Milalai, Gilalai, Maai, Nethanel, Judah, and Hanani, with the musical instruments of David, the man of God. Ezra the scribe went in front of them. At the Fountain Gate they climbed the steps of the city of David on the ascent of the wall and went above the house of David to the Water Gate on the east.

The second thanksgiving procession went to the left, and I followed it with half the people along the top of the wall, past the Tower of the Ovens to the Broad Wall, above the

Ephraim Gate, and by the Old Gate, the Fish Gate, the Tower of Hananel, and the Tower of the Hundred, to the Sheep Gate. They stopped at the Gate of the Guard.

The two thanksgiving processions stood in the house of God. So did I and half of the officials accompanying me, as well as the priests:
Eliakim, Maaseiah, Miniamin,
Micaiah, Elioenai, Zechariah,
and Hananiah, with trumpets;
and Maaseiah, Shemaiah, Eleazar,
Uzzi, Jehohanan, Malchijah, Elam, and Ezer.
Then the singers sang, with Jezrahiah as the leader. On that day they offered great sacrifices and rejoiced because God had given them great joy. The women and children also celebrated, and Jerusalem's rejoicing was heard far away.

THIRD, LEARN

Finally! It's time to celebrate the completed wall! The people have done the work bravely and with focus. They've allowed the building process to bring them closer to their God and to unite them as a country. They've received God's Law, confessed their sin, and committed to live under God's complete authority.

Party time.

And how do they party? With choirs and bands and dueling parades, culminating in a flash mob sing-a-long in the house of God. This is an EPIC party.

A few details to note:
- People are invited from far and wide, especially the Levites. They're "sought out" and "brought." This makes me think the people paid for the Levites to travel to Jerusalem for the festivities. That's important because Levites survive off the generosity of others, and it looks like Israel is keeping her vow to take care of them.
- They purify themselves before they jump into the fun. I love seeing them following God's rules and making preparations to meet Him in celebration on His terms.

This celebration is SO music-forward. Singing, a band, a choir, more singing... Clearly, there's something about music that makes a moment. In verse 36 we see the men using "the musical instruments of David." Other translations say "the musical instruments prescribed by David." These may have been the actual instruments David invented and hand-crafted. It is totally possible that on this day a man was walking the walls of the city of Jerusalem playing a Thanksgiving song, carrying a lyre David used to compose that exact song.

- What's happening with the processions or parades of choirs? They're splitting up and circling the city, meeting in the house of God. It's like they're wrapping the city in rejoicing.
- When they all arrive (in close to the same spot where they first heard the Law of Moses read aloud) they sing even more, their voices joining, commingling, intertwining. In verse 42 we get this little detail: "Then the singers sang, with Jezrahiah as the leader." We don't know much about Jezrahiah but I'm imagining he's a bit of a rock star. Nehemiah says his name for a reason—perhaps because he's a headliner (Jezrahiah was leading?! Wow. He's amazing. I love his voice.) or because Jezrahiah's name means "brightness of the Lord" or "Jehovah is shining"—perfect for the moment.
- This is a very loud party: The sound of rejoicing in Jerusalem could be heard far away.

FOURTH, REFLECT

I can't help wondering, as I watch this celebration unfold, why so few of our holiest celebrations look like this.

Why aren't we louder?

I've never marched in a holy parade—why not?

Why don't we break into song for hours?

If our God is the same God Israel worships here, offering the same joy and the same level of communal belonging and purpose, why don't we celebrate like they did? For real. Take a moment to think about it and offer a few possible reasons. Let's get this answered and fixed.

Maybe you do celebrate like this. I'd love to hear about it! Email me at jlgerhardt.godscout@gmail.com with an example.

Why do you think music is such an effective mode of celebration?

James (Jesus' brother) says to the Jerusalem church, "Is anyone happy? Let them sing songs of praise." It's not a new command; we find the injunction to rejoice in song all over the Bible.

- So, do you do it? Do you sing when you're happy? What are your go-to celebration songs? If you don't sing a lot, why do you think that is? What might help you sing more?

FIFTH, LOOK

Where do you see God in today's passage?

Why do you think God likes music so much?

Do you think God sings? (hint: Zephaniah 3:17)

What does Israel's devotion to celebration (this is the third party/celebration/holiday in a short period of time) tell us about Who God is and what He values?

Day 2

FIRST, PRAY

God, open our eyes that we might see You in your Word.
Enable us to support your work by supporting your people.

SECOND, READ

Nehemiah 12:27-47

> At the dedication of the wall of Jerusalem, they sent for the Levites wherever they lived and brought them to Jerusalem to celebrate the joyous dedication with thanksgiving and singing accompanied by cymbals, harps, and lyres. The singers gathered from the region around Jerusalem, from the settlements of the Netophathites, from Beth-gilgal, and from the fields of Geba and Azmaveth, for they had built settlements for themselves around Jerusalem. After the priests and Levites had purified themselves, they purified the people, the city gates, and the wall.
>
> Then I brought the leaders of Judah up on top of the wall, and I appointed two large processions that gave thanks. One went to the right on the wall, toward the Dung Gate. Hoshaiah and half the leaders of Judah followed, along with Azariah, Ezra, Meshullam, Judah, Benjamin, Shemaiah, Jeremiah, and some of the priests' sons with trumpets, and Zechariah son of Jonathan, son of Shemaiah, son of Mattaniah, son of Micaiah, son of Zaccur, son of Asaph followed as well as his relatives—Shemaiah, Azarel, Milalai, Gilalai, Maai, Nethanel, Judah, and Hanani, with the musical instruments of David, the man of God. Ezra the scribe went in front of them. At the Fountain Gate they climbed the steps of the city of David on the ascent of the wall and went above the house of David to the Water Gate on the east.
>
> The second thanksgiving procession went to the left, and I followed it with half the people along the top of the wall, past the Tower of the Ovens to the Broad Wall, above the

Ephraim Gate, and by the Old Gate, the Fish Gate, the Tower of Hananel, and the Tower of the Hundred, to the Sheep Gate. They stopped at the Gate of the Guard.

The two thanksgiving processions stood in the house of God. So did I and half of the officials accompanying me, as well as the priests:
Eliakim, Maaseiah, Miniamin,
Micaiah, Elioenai, Zechariah,
and Hananiah, with trumpets;
and Maaseiah, Shemaiah, Eleazar,
Uzzi, Jehohanan, Malchijah, Elam, and Ezer.

Then the singers sang, with Jezrahiah as the leader. On that day they offered great sacrifices and rejoiced because God had given them great joy. The women and children also celebrated, and Jerusalem's rejoicing was heard far away.

On that same day men were placed in charge of the rooms that housed the supplies, contributions, firstfruits, and tenths. The legally required portions for the priests and Levites were gathered from the village fields, because Judah was grateful to the priests and Levites who were serving. They performed the service of their God and the service of purification, along with the singers and gatekeepers, as David and his son Solomon had prescribed. For long ago, in the days of David and Asaph, there were heads of the singers and songs of praise and thanksgiving to God. So in the days of Zerubbabel and Nehemiah, all Israel contributed the daily portions for the singers and gatekeepers. They also set aside daily portions for the Levites, and the Levites set aside daily portions for Aaron's descendants.

THIRD, LEARN

Today's reading features the Levites. A Levite is a citizen of Israel descending from the tribe of Levi. What makes Levites unique is their lack of an inheritance and holy calling to do the work of God. Some of the Levites take care of the temple. Some work in the storerooms. Some do the work of purification, others serve as guards. And some work as musicians.

Levites can't provide for their families in the traditional way, because they haven't been given land (and because their time is devoted to the tabernacle/temple). God tells Israel in

Numbers 18:21, "I give to the Levites all the tithes in Israel as their inheritance in return for the work they do while serving at the tent of meeting."

Did you see that? 100 percent of the tithe goes to the Levites.

Here's how it works: God takes care of Israel. Israel takes care of the Levites. The Levites take care of God's temple and lead God's people in worship.

That's how it's supposed to work, but at this point in Israel's history they haven't fully returned to the law. They're working on it. Evidently, seeing the Levites in action during the celebration inspires Israel to restore the Levites to their official positions and to pay them for their work.

FOURTH, REFLECT

What would it look like for us to pay our "Levites"?

Who's making music that leads you closer to God?

Who's helping connect you to God through worship or teaching?

Who devotes him/herself fully to a holy (no-pay/low-pay) calling?

Who's the facilities or logistics person for your local church or the ministry you benefit from?

Recently I came across a Twitter thread in which hundreds of Christians complained/grumbled/railed against the idea of paying ministers. Whether or not a paid minister is the right fit for any given local church is one thing, but the idea of a paid minister is a long-standing principle among God's people. Here we see the Levites being compensated for ministry. Later in scripture we'll find Jesus himself subsisting on donations from generous followers.

Here's something that's always been true: Men and women who're called to ministry make financial sacrifices to take care of God's people. They give up the potential of lucrative work to teach, pastor, and create for the good of the kingdom. If God's people don't pay them for it, they can't do it.

Just like not having Levites was a problem for the Israelites in Nehemiah's day, a problem they realized when they saw what they were missing at the celebration, not having kingdom ministers and makers is a problem for us. And the less we contribute to their care, the fewer ministers and makers we'll have.

FIFTH, LOOK

Where do you see God in today's passage?

Why do you think God set up this way of compensating and caring for His servants? What's His heart in it?

Day 3

FIRST, PRAY

God, open our eyes that we might see You in your Word.
Empower us to live a happy ending. Give us yet another fresh start when we fail.

SECOND, READ

Nehemiah 13:1-30

> At that time the book of Moses was read publicly to the people. The command was found written in it that no Ammonite or Moabite should ever enter the assembly of God, because they did not meet the Israelites with food and water. Instead, they hired Balaam against them to curse them, but our God turned the curse into a blessing. When they heard the law, they separated all those of mixed descent from Israel.
>
> Now before this, the priest Eliashib had been put in charge of the storerooms of the house of our God. He was a relative of Tobiah and had prepared a large room for him where they had previously stored the grain offerings, the frankincense, the articles, and the tenths of grain, new wine, and fresh oil prescribed for the Levites, singers, and gatekeepers, along with the contributions for the priests.
>
> While all this was happening, I was not in Jerusalem, because I had returned to King Artaxerxes of Babylon in the thirty-second year of his reign. It was only later that I asked the king for a leave of absence so I could return to Jerusalem. Then I discovered the evil that Eliashib had done on behalf of Tobiah by providing him a room in the courts of God's house. I was greatly displeased and threw all of Tobiah's household possessions out of the room. I ordered that the rooms be purified, and I had the articles of the house of God restored there, along with the grain offering and frankincense. I also found out that because the portions for the Levites had not been given, each of the Levites and the singers performing the service had gone back to his own field. Therefore, I rebuked the officials, asking, "Why has the house of God been

135

neglected?" I gathered the Levites and singers together and stationed them at their posts. Then all Judah brought a tenth of the grain, new wine, and fresh oil into the storehouses. I appointed as treasurers over the storehouses the priest Shelemiah, the scribe Zadok, and Pedaiah of the Levites, with Hanan son of Zaccur, son of Mattaniah to assist them, because they were considered trustworthy. They were responsible for the distribution to their colleagues.

Remember me for this, my God, and don't erase the deeds of faithful love I have done for the house of my God and for its services.

At that time I saw people in Judah treading winepresses on the Sabbath. They were also bringing in stores of grain and loading them on donkeys, along with wine, grapes, and figs. All kinds of goods were being brought to Jerusalem on the Sabbath day. So I warned them against selling food on that day. The Tyrians living there were importing fish and all kinds of merchandise and selling them on the Sabbath to the people of Judah in Jerusalem.

I rebuked the nobles of Judah and said to them, "What is this evil you are doing— profaning the Sabbath day? Didn't your ancestors do the same, so that our God brought all this disaster on us and on this city? And now you are rekindling his anger against Israel by profaning the Sabbath!

When shadows began to fall on the city gates of Jerusalem just before the Sabbath, I gave orders that the city gates be closed and not opened until after the Sabbath. I posted some of my men at the gates, so that no goods could enter during the Sabbath day. Once or twice the merchants and those who sell all kinds of goods camped outside Jerusalem, but I warned them, "Why are you camping in front of the wall? If you do it again, I'll use force against you." After that they did not come again on the Sabbath. Then I instructed the Levites to purify themselves and guard the city gates in order to keep the Sabbath day holy.

Remember me for this also, my God, and look on me with compassion according to the abundance of your faithful love.

In those days I also saw Jews who had married women from Ashdod, Ammon, and Moab. Half of their children spoke the language of Ashdod or the language of one of the other peoples but could not speak Hebrew. I rebuked them, cursed them, beat some of their men, and pulled out their hair. I forced them to take an oath before God and said, "You must not give your daughters in marriage to their sons or take their daughters as wives for your sons or yourselves! Didn't King Solomon of Israel sin in matters like this? There was not a king like him among many nations. He was loved by his God, and God made him king over all Israel, yet foreign women drew him into sin. Why then should we hear about you doing all this terrible evil and acting unfaithfully against our God by marrying foreign women?" Even one of the sons of Jehoiada, son of the high priest Eliashib, had become a son-in-law to Sanballat the Horonite. So I drove him away from me.

Remember them, my God, for defiling the priesthood as well as the covenant of the priesthood and the Levites.

So I purified them from everything foreign and assigned specific duties to each of the priests and Levites.

THIRD, LEARN

We'll spend the next three days going over what's happening here in Nehemiah 13 (explaining some of the harder to understand details), but for today, here's what I want to notice: This is the ending to the book of Nehemiah. *And it is the worst.*

Nehemiah opens with our hero grieving over a ruined Jerusalem. If Nehemiah ended at verse 47 of chapter 12, we'd have closed the story with our hero celebrating a rebuilt Jerusalem, a city following the law and flourishing. The plot of the story would be the plot we love: Hero sets out on quest to save the world. Hero overcomes obstacles to save the world. Hero saves the world. Everyone celebrates (this plot structure works pretty well either with Nehemiah cast as the hero or with God as the hero).

Instead, we end with chapter 13. Nehemiah has returned to Jerusalem after time away (he had to report back to his boss in Persia). Scholars disagree on how long Nehemiah's gone— perhaps a little over a year, perhaps 15 years. We don't know. What we do know is what Nehemiah finds when he returns: an Israel that has failed to keep the oaths they made to God. They've neglected the house of God, failed to pay the Levites, intermarried with the surrounding nations, and failed to keep the Sabbath. For Nehemiah, who dedicated so much of his life to restoring Jerusalem to its ancient glory, this is catastrophic.

We can see that in his reaction. He purges the temple of Tobiah's possessions (imagine an angry wife throwing her unfaithful husband's clothes on the front lawn). He rebukes the officials. He warns and preaches and reminds and commands. At one point he seems to lose himself completely: "I rebuked them, cursed them, beat some of their men, and pulled out their hair." Later he'll drive a guy out of the community.

Nehemiah isn't only angry. He also goes to work repairing and re-orienting. He can't help it; he's compelled to fix what's broken (totally an enneagram 1).

Did he fix it? Is everything better for Israel from this point on? *I think you know the answer.*

We suspect the book of Malachi was written during this phase of Israel's history, and in it we get a glimpse at both Israel's defiance and God's faithfulness. God (ever-compassionate) says, "I the Lord do not change. So you, the descendants of Jacob, are not destroyed. Ever since the time of your ancestors you have turned away from my decrees and have not kept them. Return to me, and I will return to you" (Malachi 3:6-7, NIV).

From what we know of the next 400 years of Israel's history (the intertestamental period), they never did fully return to God.

FOURTH, REFLECT

I keep asking myself, "Why would God end the story this way?" Why not end with the celebration—the happier ending?

I think the answer is this: God tells the truth. The whole truth. Even when it's unflattering or sad or "bad storytelling."

Yes, Israel will receive another opportunity for a happy ending—in the form of Jesus Christ—but for now, the story ends with broken oaths.

Clearly, though He hates them, God allows unhappy endings. He allows His people to choose against Him.

What does that mean to you? How does it affect you?

Are you choosing an unhappy ending? Do you love someone who's choosing an unhappy ending? Spend some time in prayer asking God to call you or your loved one home. Ask Him to make you strong for the journey.

FIFTH, LOOK

Where do you see God in today's passage?

What does this ending to the book of Nehemiah reveal about the nature or character of God? What other examples do we find in scripture of God choosing to tell the true story over the "happy" one?

Day 4

FIRST, PRAY

God, open our eyes that we might see You in your Word.
Empower us to follow the rules, because our hearts follow You.

SECOND, READ

Nehemiah 13:1-30

At that time the book of Moses was read publicly to the people. The command was found written in it that no Ammonite or Moabite should ever enter the assembly of God, because they did not meet the Israelites with food and water. Instead, they hired Balaam against them to curse them, but our God turned the curse into a blessing. When they heard the law, they separated all those of mixed descent from Israel.
Now before this, the priest Eliashib had been put in charge of the storerooms of the house of our God. He was a relative of Tobiah and had prepared a large room for him where they had previously stored the grain offerings, the frankincense, the articles, and the tenths of grain, new wine, and fresh oil prescribed for the Levites, singers, and gatekeepers, along with the contributions for the priests.

While all this was happening, I was not in Jerusalem, because I had returned to King Artaxerxes of Babylon in the thirty-second year of his reign. It was only later that I asked the king for a leave of absence so I could return to Jerusalem. Then I discovered the evil that Eliashib had done on behalf of Tobiah by providing him a room in the courts of God's house. I was greatly displeased and threw all of Tobiah's household possessions out of the room. I ordered that the rooms be purified, and I had the articles of the house of God restored there, along with the grain offering and frankincense. I also found out that because the portions for the Levites had not been given, each of the Levites and the singers performing the service had gone back to his own field. Therefore, I rebuked the officials, asking, "Why has the house of God been neglected?" I gathered the Levites and singers together and stationed them at their posts. Then all Judah brought a tenth of the grain, new wine, and fresh oil into the storehouses. I appointed as treasurers over the storehouses the priest Shelemiah, the scribe Zadok, and Pedaiah of the Levites, with Hanan son of Zaccur, son of Mattaniah to assist them, because they were considered trustworthy. They were responsible for the distribution to their colleagues. Remember me for this, my God, and don't erase the deeds of faithful love I have done for the house of my God and for its services.

At that time I saw people in Judah treading winepresses on the Sabbath. They were also bringing in stores of grain and loading them on donkeys, along with wine, grapes, and figs. All kinds of goods were being brought to Jerusalem on the Sabbath day. So I warned them against selling food on that day. The Tyrians living there were importing fish and all kinds of merchandise and selling them on the Sabbath to the people of Judah in Jerusalem.

I rebuked the nobles of Judah and said to them, "What is this evil you are doing— profaning the Sabbath day? Didn't your ancestors do the same, so that our God brought all this disaster on us and on this city? And now you are rekindling his anger against Israel by profaning the Sabbath!

When shadows began to fall on the city gates of Jerusalem just before the Sabbath, I gave orders that the city gates be closed and not opened until after the Sabbath. I posted some of my men at the gates, so that no goods could enter during the Sabbath day. Once or twice the merchants and those who sell all kinds of goods camped outside Jerusalem, but I warned them, "Why are you camping in front of the wall? If you do it again, I'll use force against you." After that they did not come again on the Sabbath. Then I instructed the Levites to purify themselves and guard the city gates in order to keep the Sabbath day holy.

Remember me for this also, my God, and look on me with compassion according to the abundance of your faithful love.

In those days I also saw Jews who had married women from Ashdod, Ammon, and Moab. Half of their children spoke the language of Ashdod or the language of one of the other peoples but could not speak Hebrew. I rebuked them, cursed them, beat some of their men, and pulled out their hair. I forced them to take an oath before God and said, "You must not give your daughters in marriage to their sons or take their daughters as wives for your sons or yourselves! Didn't King Solomon of Israel sin in matters like this? There was not a king like him among many nations. He was loved by his God, and God made him king over all Israel, yet foreign women drew him into sin. Why then should we hear about you doing all this terrible evil and acting unfaithfully against our God by marrying foreign women?" Even one of the sons of Jehoiada, son of the high priest Eliashib, had become a son-in-law to Sanballat the Horonite. So I drove him away from me.

Remember them, my God, for defiling the priesthood as well as the covenant of the priesthood and the Levites.

So I purified them from everything foreign and assigned specific duties to each of the priests and Levites.

THIRD, LEARN

Today, let's work through the broken commands and see what they reveal about Israel's relationship with God:

- In verses 1-9 we discover that Israel has disobeyed the command to never let an Ammonite or Moabite into the assembly by welcoming Tobiah (of all people!) into the temple and giving him a spare room. Tobiah appears to have connections to one of the priests (maybe they're related, maybe they've had business dealings, maybe they went to high school together). Nehemiah discovers Tobiah and throws him out.
  - This command grows out of a past encounter with the Ammonites and Moabites recorded in Numbers chapters 21-24 in which, lusty for blood, the nearby nations refuse to let Israel pass by peacefully. If you haven't read the story of Balaam, hired by Israel's enemies to curse them, check it out. One of the star characters is a talking donkey!
  - Why would God forbid the Ammonites and Moabites from EVER entering the assembly of God? We don't know—God's prerogative. Perhaps he's protecting Israel from their influence. Perhaps they're marked by unrepentant generational sin, unclean and unable to stand in God's presence.
  - What about this question: What does Israel's breaking of the command reveal about Israel? This is one of those commands that's about loyalty. To whom is Israel devoted? The nations who betrayed them and cursed them? Or their God who is ever faithful?

- The Levites aren't paid and the house of God is neglected.
  - This seems like simple greedy selfishness. The people kept for themselves what was owed to God. Refusal to tithe finds its roots in distrust of God and a prioritization of personal welfare over God's instructions.
- Working on the Sabbath.
  - Working on the Sabbath ultimately reflects a lack of trust in God for provision or a dissatisfaction with God's provision. People who can't stop working to observe commanded rest are either people who feel like they need to provide for themselves or people who never have enough. Either way, working on the Sabbath is a clear message: I need more than God provides.
- Marrying foreign women.
  - Nehemiah says about marrying women from the surrounding nations, "Didn't King Solomon of Israel sin in matters like this? There was not a king like him among many nations. He was loved by his God, and God made him king over all Israel, yet foreign women drew him into sin." If Solomon could be led away from God by his wives, who can withstand the temptation?
  - Nehemiah's explanation makes it clear: God doesn't want Israel marrying foreign women (or men) because God wants Israel to stay faithful to worshiping Him, and the foreign influence to pursue idolatry is too strong to fight against.
  - Israel's decision to marry into foreign nations makes it clear: Israel isn't looking for an exclusive relationship with Jehovah. They'd prefer something more open.

FOURTH, REFLECT

Every one of these broken commands and disobedient behaviors reveals something deeper about Israel's heart. These moments represent a lack of loyalty and split devotion. They reveal deep selfishness and greed. They manifest a lack of trust in God as provider and a refusal to exclusively follow the way of God.

- Are you struggling right now to follow any of God's commands? What's the deeper issue? What does your disobedience reveal about your relationship with God?

FIFTH, LOOK

Where do you see God in today's passage?

What do the rules God made reveal about Who God is?

Why does He want Israel to follow these rules?

Day 5

FIRST, PRAY

God, open our eyes that we might see You in your Word.
Remember us with favor.

SECOND, READ

Nehemiah 13:1-30 (focusing on verses 6-10, 14-18, 22-25, & 29-31)

6-10
While all this was happening, I was not in Jerusalem, because I had returned to King Artaxerxes of Babylon in the thirty-second year of his reign. It was only later that I asked the king for a leave of absence so I could return to Jerusalem. Then I discovered the evil that Eliashib had done on behalf of Tobiah by providing him a room in the courts of God's house. I was greatly displeased and threw all of Tobiah's household possessions out of the room. I ordered that the rooms be purified, and I had the articles of the house of God restored there, along with the grain offering and frankincense. I also found out that because the portions for the Levites had not been given, each of the Levites and the singers performing the service had gone back to his own field.

14-18
Remember me for this, my God, and don't erase the deeds of faithful love I have done for the house of my God and for its services.
At that time I saw people in Judah treading winepresses on the Sabbath. They were also bringing in stores of grain and loading them on donkeys, along with wine, grapes, and figs. All kinds of goods were being brought to Jerusalem on the Sabbath day. So I warned them against selling food on that day. The Tyrians living there were importing fish and all kinds of merchandise and selling them on the Sabbath to the people of Judah in Jerusalem.
I rebuked the nobles of Judah and said to them, "What is this evil you are doing—profaning the Sabbath day? Didn't your ancestors do the same, so that our God

brought all this disaster on us and on this city? And now you are rekindling his anger against Israel by profaning the Sabbath!"

22-25

Then I instructed the Levites to purify themselves and guard the city gates in order to keep the Sabbath day holy.

Remember me for this also, my God, and look on me with compassion according to the abundance of your faithful love.

In those days I also saw Jews who had married women from Ashdod, Ammon, and Moab. Half of their children spoke the language of Ashdod or the language of one of the other peoples but could not speak Hebrew.

I rebuked them, cursed them, beat some of their men, and pulled out their hair. I forced them to take an oath before God and said, "You must not give your daughters in marriage to their sons or take their daughters as wives for your sons or yourselves!"

29-31

Remember them, my God, for defiling the priesthood as well as the covenant of the priesthood and the Levites.

So I purified them from everything foreign and assigned specific duties to each of the priests and Levites. I also arranged for the donation of wood at the appointed times and for the firstfruits.

Remember me, my God, with favor.

THIRD, LEARN

Throughout the book of Nehemiah, the man Nehemiah faithfully partners with Israel to build both the wall and a law-abiding community of God followers. Though he's clearly the leader, he's also a team player, recognizing that God's people rise and fall together.

When the book opens we find Nehemiah praying this prayer:

"Let your ear be attentive and your eyes open to hear the prayer your servant is praying before you day and night for your servants, the people of Israel. I confess the sins we Israelites, including myself and my father's family, have committed against you. We have acted very wickedly toward you. We have not obeyed the commands, decrees and laws you gave your servant Moses...

Lord, let your ear be attentive to the prayer of this your servant and to the prayer of your servants who delight in revering your name."

Nehemiah prays for "we Israelites."

As the book closes we can't help but notice a shift in Nehemiah's prayers. Three times he prays in chapter 13:

- "Remember me for this, my God, and don't erase the deeds of faithful love I have done for the house of my God and for its services" (vs 14).
- "Remember me for this also, my God, and look on me with compassion according to the abundance of your faithful love." (vs 22).
- "Remember me, my God, with favor" (vs 31).

Nehemiah seems to be distancing himself from the choices made by Israel, choices he knows undo the oath and deserve punishment, asking God to remember ME, not us.

This is a much bigger deal than you or I (western, modern readers) can understand.

In the book *Misreading Scripture with Western Eyes: Removing Cultural Blinders to Better Understand the Bible*, Brandon J O'Brien and E. Richards contrast the west and east as individualistic and collectivist cultures. They write, "Western societies are, by and large, individualistic societies. The most important entity in an individualistic culture is the individual person." Conversely, "Members of collectivist cultures make decisions based on the counsel of elders—parents, aunts or uncles. The highest goal and virtue in this sort of culture is supporting the community."

Nehemiah is born a collectivist. His highest value is supporting the community. And yet, after years of devoting himself to Israel, he finds himself in a place where he simply cares more about God's favor than He does about Israel's favor.

If Israel refuses to follow God, Nehemiah will refuse to follow Israel.

FOURTH, REFELCT

This ending is sad as it reflects the deterioration of Nehemiah's relationship with His people. But it's also beautiful as it reflects the depth of Nehemiah's relationship with his God.

Nehemiah holds nothing back as he wages war against disobedience to the law. He's devoted to keeping God's commands even when his devotion might make him unpopular with the people, even when it makes him feel alone.

- Have you ever been unpopular with people because of your devotion to God? Was it worth it?

- How do we remind ourselves that a relationship with God matters even more than a relationship with people? Is there a prayer we could pray? A spiritual practice?

- What similarities do you see between Nehemiah and Jesus? How might Nehemiah help us understand God?

- Again and again Nehemiah asks God to "Remember me." When/why does Nehemiah want God to remember Him? What will be different if God remembers Nehemiah with favor?

FIFTH, LOOK

My hope is that this study has drawn you closer to God, that you've seen Him more clearly and in seeing Him have come to know and love Him better.

Where have you seen God in the book of Nehemiah?

Who is He? What does He care about?

Take some time today to pray, talking to God about what you've learned about Him.

Say,

"God, You are _____ and _____ and _____."

"God, You always _____"

"God, You never _____"

Then tell God what you're wondering about Him. What do you wish He'd make clearer? What do you struggle to understand?

Finally, thank Him for Who He is.

TAKE A FEW MINUTES AND WATCH OUR LAST TEACHING VIDEO AT JLGERHARDT.COM/FRESHSTART. THIS WEEK WE'RE TALKING ABOUT HOW TO THROW AN EPIC PARTY AND HOW NOT TO END AN STORY.

Remember me,

... look on me with compassion

according to the abundance of your

faithful love

NEHEMIAH 13:22

EPILOGUE

I decided to study the book of Nehemiah because the world around me was crumbling. Everything broken? Read a book about rebuilding!

What I found was a God who never gives up on His people and, in the person of Nehemiah, a human being who refuses to give up on his God.

I came looking for advice, and I stumbled upon a love story.

That's so often the case with Bible study; we come seeking to know things or improve ourselves, and we discover, if we're looking closely, an invitation to be loved by a God with "abundant compassion."

I hope you've learned things as you've read the book of Nehemiah. I hope you've been challenged to change the way you live. But most importantly, I hope you've seen God, and I hope that in seeing Him up close you've fallen even more deeply in love.

APPENDIX A

Timeline of Events Leading Up to Nehemiah

BABYLON DESTROYS THE TEMPLE

586 BC

598 BC

BABYLON TAKES 1ST WAVE OF
ISRAELITES INTO EXILE

ZERUBBABEL LEADS 1ST WAVE
OF EXILE RETURN

538 BC

539 BC

FALL OF BABYLON TO PERSIA

WORK ON TEMPLE BEGINS

536 BC

537 BC

BUILDING OF THE ALTAR

WORK ON TEMPLE RESUMES UNDER
DARIUS & EVENTS OF THE
BOOKS OF HAGGAI & ZECHARIAH

520-518 BC

530-520 BC

WORK ON TEMPLE CEASES

EVENTS OF THE BOOK OF ESTHER

483-471 BC

516 BC

TEMPLE COMPLETED

444 BC

NEHEMIAH RETURNS TO
JERUSALEM

ABOUT THE AUTHOR

JL Gerhardt is the author of six books including *Think Good* and *Prayer, In Practice.* She currently lives nomadically, wandering the globe with her husband and two daughters, seeking God's face in new places and new people.

Gerhardt loves swimming in cold water, family dance parties, and the sound of her husband nearby singing and playing guitar while she drinks coffee and reads books.

If you're interested in having JL speak at your seminar, retreat, or conference, visit jlgerhardt.com/speaking.

This is the first Bible study in her *Look To Love* series.

Subscribe!

Subscribe to JL Gerhardt's FREE semimonthly email, The Goodness--essays on seeking and seeing God & prompts for purposeful encounters. Like David in Psalm 27 ("I remain confident of this: I will see the goodness of the Lord in the land of the living") and Moses before him who met God "face to face," radiant light dripping from his pores as he walked away, Gerhardt thinks looking at God is as good as it gets. She writes thoughtfully about what she sees and how she sees it, offering wise counsel to anyone open to looking.

"JL shines light into the dark places like someone with a headlamp crawling through a cave. She illuminates any space she gazes upon. Lucky for us she takes a look at the hard stuff: Grief. Doubt. Faith fatigue. Ego. Religion. Parenting..."

-reader Carly Cross

JLGERHARDT.SUBSTACK.COM

Made in the USA
Monee, IL
07 June 2021